I Wish
He'd Taught Me
How to Shave

I Wish
He'd Taught Me
How to Shave

DAVE LANDERS, PhD

Contents

Acknowledgments

I admit that I am one of those readers who *do* read acknowledgements at the beginning of books; I also stay in the movie theater until the end to read the credits as they scroll across the screen—curious to learn who helped an author or filmmaker complete their work. Now I know.

Over many years, this book has grown from a kernel of an idea into what you now hold in your hands; I cannot begin to thank my Saint Michael's College students adequately—all of them—for believing in me and for trusting themselves and me enough to share their essays here. They said that they wanted to make a difference and wanted their voices and experiences to be heard; I trust that this book does just that. Students, thanks also for your social media and book marketing support; ten years ago, I had no clue as to the power of Facebook—now I rely on it and all of you to get the word out.

Thank you Bryan Burkhard for agreeing, without hesitation, to pose for the book's front cover photo; thank you to both Bryan and Rudyard Colter for the back cover. To my nephew Brian, who is mentioned and pictured in the book with his son Bodhi (my great-nephew), thank you for asking "that father question" so many years ago. Bodhi is very lucky to have you for his father and Marisol for his mother.

Paul Sapia and Liz Siekman—your encouragement has meant the world to me.

Thank you "Ben" for your essay containing what proved to be the book title, for many wonderful conversations, and for continuing to challenge yourself to deal with the issues raised in that essay. The energy and enthusiasm you and your girlfriend brought to this project have been more supportive than you may ever know.

A number of my Saint Michael's College colleagues have provided me with helpful and timely advice—Traci Griffith, Jon Hyde, and Kimberly Sultze from our Media Studies and Digital Arts Department—thank you for your time and wise counsel. Fr. Mike, Jennie and Art, Sue, Ann and Karen and Paul—our group provides much needed support for anyone struggling to work full time *and* have a book published. Caroline Crawford, friend, and colleague, thank you for your advice. Jack Neuhauser, president of Saint Michael's—thank you for your friendship and support.

The initial readers of drafts—Davis and Ann Clark, Craig and Colleen Farnum, Sue and Jim Wall—your careful advice was invaluable. Maggie Wall—your wise counsel on the cover of the book was helpful, and although busy, I always know that you are there for support. Jim Howland, Brian Moore, Tom Robinson—thanks for timely advice and assistance.

Janet DeMars and Craig Farnum, thank you for a successful collaboration that allowed me to work with your clients at Jaywalker Lodge in Carbondale, Colorado. Until participating in those workshops, I had not thought of the recovery community as one that could/would benefit from this book—your initiative has launched an outstanding program.

Craig Mitchell and Kim-Quinn Smith—your love and support throughout this entire venture have been incredible. Your words of wisdom, your unconditional help, and willingness to "be there" are very much appreciated. Craig, I am and always will be proud when you call me "Dad."

To all of the folks at Wind Ridge Books of Vermont (WRBV) who took a chance on me with their agreement to publish this book—a huge thank you. To my doctor and friend, Frank Landry who joins my Men & Masculinities class each spring to talk about men's health issues, thank you for first suggesting that I contact Wind Ridge's Publisher, Holly Johnson. Thank you to WRBV's editors, Lin Stone and Emily Copeland; their direction and encouragement have been remarkable. Thanks to the gifted artistic team, "Brit" Craig Thomas and his partner, Molly Stone-Thomas for the brilliant photographs and cleverly executed videos. Thank you to Laurie Thomas for the elegant book design. Thank you one and all for such steadfast encouragement and support.

To my family—to my sister Sue and her husband Jim Wall and their two "kids" Maggie and Mike Wall—thank you for the great gift of loving acceptance; I am grateful daily. Finally, Mom, I know you would be proud, and Dad, I know you would never understand, but I also know you both did the best job you knew how to do. Thank you.

Introduction

"I just wish he had taught me how to shave."
—Ben, 22

I was fifteen when my father died. He was recuperating at home from a recent heart attack, and while Mom worked down the street at a neighbor's roofing company as a part-time accountant, my job that day was to "watch your father" as he rested on the porch. He and I had not had a good relationship, and in fact, we'd had a fight the day before. I had vowed that I wasn't going to speak to him again until he apologized for yelling at me for some meaningless thing. When Mom came rushing into the house telling me, "Go get Dr. Flo—I think your father is dead," I knew that things were never going to be the same again. Our doctor lived across the street, and as I flew off the porch toward her house, I glimpsed my dad seemingly asleep in his lounge chair on the porch—in the same position he had been in every time I looked out the dining-room window.

His death solidly and profoundly affected all of us; life truly never was the same again. My oldest brother was in the Navy and was at sea at the time. When he called to arrange to be home for the funeral, his first question was, "How is Dave?" It was as if he knew that out of the four children, I would take Dad's death the hardest. I was always the "sensitive" one. This concern for me struck me as a special thing; my brother showed more care than I had ever felt from our father.

As the youngest of the three boys in my family with a younger sister, I never understood whether I was different because my father didn't love me or if he didn't love me because I was different. Unlike my brothers, I wasn't into sports; I did well in school and got my first library card at age four. Dad had a ninth-grade education and couldn't understand my love of reading—nor much of anything else about me. After his death, I was not allowed to attend the funeral or the burial and was taken to the funeral home for a viewing when no others would be around. No one ever explained any of this to me; even though I was fifteen years old, I was treated as if I were a mere child.

I have found in my many years of working with young people that this "not explaining things" is pervasive in our society. For some reason, we don't share the truth with our children, and sadly, that leaves them, as it did me, with many more questions than answers. What was wrong with me? is most often what young people ask me about their young selves. Because no one is straightforward or honest with children about "adult" issues, the assumption children often make is that there must be something wrong with them.

I have my PhD from Wayne State University in Detroit in educational counseling. People have always told me that I am easy to talk to, and I suspect that my educational choices were a bit of an attempt to try to "be there" for others, because no one had seemingly ever "been there" for me. I want young people to have someone who believes in them and who can help them understand just how good they really are—how there is nothing wrong with them. Teachers and counselors who work with young people get to see and hear about the pain that so many young men and women carry unnecessarily. Many, many of my students have been looking for some type of validation that they never felt they had at home—especially from a father. Most blame themselves. Many make excuses like I had done at one point: "He works hard all day so doesn't have time for me." Many simply accept that their father was not someone with whom they could ever become close. Many question themselves rather than be "disloyal" to their father. Too many learned early on how to be a father from their fathers, for better or worse.

For years I have had students tell me that they love their fathers and appreciate all that they have done and provided for them—the homes, the education, the family trips, et cetera. And perhaps fathers have done these things because that is what they think is expected of them. But at the same time, I can't count the number of times students have said, I just wish he was there for my cross-country meet; or I just wish he was there to teach me how to shave; or I just wish he was there to play catch in the backyard. How do we get fathers to understand this? We need to do a better job of communicating to fathers that perhaps the job of "being there" is more important than what society has been telling them to do—namely: provide,

provide. Additionally, fathers need to be able to let their kids know why they are not there and that it isn't because "I don't want to be," or that "I don't care or love you," or that "There is something wrong with you." An open dialogue can do much to prevent destructive insecurity and self-blame on the part of the child.

Guilt is a powerful emotion, perhaps one of the most powerful—right up there with shame. Guilt is when you think you have done something wrong and shame is when you are the something that is wrong. I carried a lot of guilt and not a little shame for years over the day my father died on our front porch. While no one ever said that I should have done anything differently, I will always wonder (even though he has been dead now for over fifty years) if I should or could have done anything differently. It's hard not to wonder how my life would have changed had I truly done a better job at "watch your father." But I also know that guilt is a wasted emotion, and I try to have my students understand this concept too.

Before moving to Vermont, I was a counselor in the public schools of Pontiac, Michigan, for sixteen years. I worked with hundreds of young people, and family tensions were part of my everyday life. When I first came to Vermont and Saint Michael's College, I was the director of the Student Resource Center, which provided all of the career development and personal counseling for the small Catholic college. I was also one of the personal counselors. For twenty-three years, much as I had done in Pontiac, I sat in my office and listened to my students. I listened to their pain, and I listened to them question their own worth. But mostly, I listened to them desperately seek validation—even if it was from a stranger with the title of counselor.

For the past twelve years, I have been teaching a course called Men & Masculinities. This course is an outgrowth of other gender studies courses I have taught (or team-taught) at St. Mike's. One year, all of us who were teaching gender studies courses came together to discuss our curriculum, and one of the things that came out of that meeting was a need for a course that dealt specifically with men's issues. Men & Masculinities is the only course in the Gender Studies major/minor that deals specifically with men's issues, and it is the only course (by design) that has a specified balance of the sexes—fifteen men and fifteen women. It meets for three hours, one night a week. Initially, the course was open to everyone, and I had two brothers who took it, a brother/sister combination, an engaged couple, and a good mix of sophomores, juniors, and seniors. As the course grew in popularity, I was forced to limit the course to thirty seniors, and I now have a waitlist of more than forty students each semester. I have sophomores approach me asking to have their names placed on the waitlist! And while this is a good thing, it also shows that there is more of an interest in this topic than most would assume. I often get reactions such as, "There are girls [sic] who take this course?" "You have a waitlist that long?" "Men actually sign up for this course?" I also get several colleagues each year who ask if they can come and visit the class at some point in the semester. My response is always the same: I am happy for the interest, but the dynamic of the course precludes visitors. I also find that many of my colleagues, aware of my passion for and interest in men's issues, come to my office to chat about their own issues. Often they want me to help them better understand their own children (usually their sons) or their own fathers.

We cover a wide array of topics in Men & Masculinities, ranging from men's health to the hopes, fears, and dreams of the specific seniors in the class. Some of the topics are more traditionally academic, others are dictated by the times we live in; some of the topics are things that I am particularly passionate about, and some are the result of workshops or conferences that I have attended. There is a good deal of literature out there on men's issues. In particular, Michael Kimmel and William Pollack have done excellent work on issues of understanding men and boys. At one conference, I heard Terrence Real speak about fathers and about his book *I Don't Want to Talk About It*, which deals not with alexithymia (an inability to understand/express emotions) but with how the clinical definition of depression might just be different for men than for women. I made his book required reading for Men & Masculinities and had student after student tell me that the men in Real's book were just like their fathers. It was after getting this reaction that I began the assignment that led to this book: I decided to see how well my students understood their fathers' role in the social construction of What Is a Man?

Much of what I heard at the academic conferences about masculinity supported my own experiences with my students and my own family, and yet, there was also something lacking. All of the theory in the world cannot help that young man or that young woman asking himself or herself, "What is wrong with me?" Several stories of father-son relationships illustrate the importance of addressing this insecurity and are at the heart of why I chose to take on the project of collecting answers to the question of what makes a man a man.

▶ Brian

I remember visiting my brother and his family one summer. My nephew Brian was ten at the time of this particular visit, and I stayed in the attic, which was his domain. I would have been content to sleep on the floor, but my nephew gave me his bed. I always enjoyed talking with Brian; he was a really nice kid and now he is a wonderful man. Back when I shared the attic with him, I was about to drop off to sleep when he asked me, "Uncle Dave, how come Dad never plays catch with me in the backyard like my friends' dads do?"

Is the measure of a man whether or not he plays catch with his son in the backyard? I suppose for some young men it is. I told Brian that it wasn't that his dad—my brother—didn't love him, it was simply that our father had never done that with us, and so perhaps my brother had never realized that this was something that should have been done. I tried to explain to this sweet ten year old that our father (his grandfather) had been a mailman who worked really, really hard, came home from work tired, and never had the time to go out and play catch with us. The reality and the truth was that our father came home from work around five-thirty and went straight upstairs to his bedroom where he "took a nap" before dinner. Mom never started dinner until Dad was home—a fact that made no sense back then, but now it does. What we didn't know or understand then was that Dad got off work at three in the afternoon and spent the next two hours drinking with his friends at the local American Legion Post. Dad hadn't been a veteran of any war, but he knew all the men there (the American Legion Post was part of his mail route). He was an outgoing and funny guy, and the American Legion was where he chose to spend several hours each day before heading home to his wife and four kids. Of course, that also meant that when he did get home, he was drunk. But we never knew that back then, we just knew that Dad was tired from working so hard as a mailman, walking his route every day. Naturally, Mom never explained this to any of us. She merely waited until he got home. She also sent me upstairs to wake him up when dinner was ready. (To this day, the smell of cigarettes, alcohol, and sweat is difficult for me to stomach.) I would shake him and tell him, "Dinner is ready," and he would either not respond or yell at me. I never understood that it was the alcohol doing the talking. I took it personally and hated being asked to wake him up every day. I would return downstairs and dutifully tell my mother that I had told him. Then when it was time for food to be put on the table, I had to truck back up the stairs to face him and his wrath and his smells and tell him that dinner was on the table.

Today, I wish that Mom had done things differently, but she didn't, and I ended up with more than a few issues over that daily routine. It is important, however, to share information with children when it is age appropriate: I chose not to tell ten-year-old Brian that his grandfather was a drunk and so he never played catch with his sons in the backyard, either.

Brian is a father now. As I first began this book, I wondered whether he plays catch with his son. With the advent of Facebook, I actually get to follow Brian and his family, and I know that he is a good dad. He talks with his son, he walks with his son, he listens to his son, he loves his son, and he learns from his son. He recently posted the following, and I share it with his permission: "I woke up today with my son saying, 'You are the best dad that a son could ever have.' After pointing out that he was the best son a dad could have, the self-reflection kicked in. Am I the best me that I can be? I always get hit with the Rush lyric of, 'Seems to me I can live my life a lot better than I think I am!' There is work to do. . . ."

For me, the sad thing about this particular story is that Brian, much like so many of the young men I have worked with over the years, initially thought that there must be something wrong with him because his dad didn't play catch with him in the backyard. The reality, however, was that his dad didn't because his dad didn't and probably, his dad didn't, either. The cyclical nature of familial relationships resulted in a ten year old wondering if there was something wrong with him. And had he not raised that question with his uncle, he might have carried that "there's something wrong with me" for a lifetime. Here's hoping he hasn't.

Brian's question about why his father hadn't played ball with him in the backyard reminds me of Frank, a friend who asked such a strong and gut-wrenching question that his story also provided me with some incentive to write this book.

▶ Frank

I went kayaking with a man whom I have known for his whole life. His father had just been diagnosed with stage IV lung cancer, and I wanted to see how he was doing with the recent diagnosis. Frank's own twenty-year-old son had been killed in a car accident a year and a half earlier, so I knew that all of this would be very difficult for him. I chose to invite him kayaking because of the sage advice offered by researcher and author William Pollack, whose book *Real Boys* has been a cornerstone of my work and a staple in my classes for many years. Pollack writes: "Rather than nudging a boy to sit down and share his feelings . . . begin by simply joining him in an activity that he enjoys. Often by simply doing something with the boy—playing a game with him, joining him for a duet on the piano, taking him to an amusement park—we forge a connection that then enables him to open up. In the middle of the game, the duet, or the Ferris wheel ride, a boy may often feel close and safe enough to share the feelings he'd otherwise keep hidden."

Pollack's advice to do something with boys to forge a bond had rung true in the case of a former student of mine, who was asked by the student newspaper to speak about a member of the community who had been significant in his life. He mentioned me. He said that, while he had never set foot in my counseling office for a counseling session, I had been his counselor for two years; we played racquetball regularly on campus and we talked before games, between games, and after games. He was someone who wouldn't "go for counseling" but who benefited from talking while doing something.

It was this method of talking-while-doing that I hoped would help Frank in this difficult time. As we began our paddle, Frank said, "I don't think I've dealt with my son's death yet, much less my dad's diagnosis." I assured him that with time he would begin to deal with both things. He turned in his kayak and said quietly, "Sometimes I wonder, was I a good father?"

What a powerful question, and not one that easily gets asked or answered. We talked about what Frank's relationship had been like with his son. While he acknowledged that he had not always done or said the right things, he did recognize that "I must have done some things right because he was such a good kid."

Do all fathers ask that question at some point? Do all fathers wonder if they are doing a good job as a dad? Who do you ask if you do have those thoughts and questions? I was glad that he could ask me, and that we could talk about it. Frank's father died several months later, and there was no doubt that he saw his father, even with his flaws, as a good father—and he told him that before he died.

▶ Henry

A good friend of mine, Henry, was concerned that he and his son were not as close as he would like them to be. I suggested that he ask his son about this, and he did. While they were driving, Henry asked his son if he was happy with their relationship. To his credit, Henry's son said, "No," and that he would like to spend more time with his dad. Because my friend was able to take the risk of asking his son a difficult question, they had a great opportunity for an open, honest conversation. I wonder just how many fathers ever ask this question, and how many sons give an honest answer if and when the question is asked in the first place.

Later, Henry was at the White House because his company was being honored along with several other companies for its work in the area of women's health issues. After the ceremony was complete, Henry asked a White House aide if it could be arranged for him to get to the airport as soon as possible. The aide informed him that they were about to move to the Rose Garden for photos with the First Lady. My friend said simply that he had to get home because it was Halloween, and he wanted to take his kids trick-or-treating. Henry knew that it was more important for him (and his two kids) to be home instead of posing for pictures—even with the First Lady.

There is such a strong connection between the social constructions of what makes a man a man and what the role of a father is. Early on in Men & Masculinities, I assigned the following paper topic: How My Father Influenced My View of What a Man Is. The papers were incredible. Students poured out their emotions, their fears, their celebrations, their hopes, and their disappointments about their fathers—often for the first time. Women told me that they wanted their partners to be just like their dads or absolutely nothing like their dads. Men told me how their fathers treated them and how their views of being a man were so often modeled after their dads. The connection between being a man and being a father seemed inextricable. I had students tell me that they had seldom, if ever, seen their fathers cry (except at the funeral of their own mother or father). And if any fathers had served in the military during the Vietnam War or the Gulf War, none of them ever talked about that experience. Their fathers didn't teach them about sex, but they often taught them about alcohol. I kept the papers, asking each semester if I could retain them. I hoped someday I could use their good works for a book or an article. The students all gave permission: This book is a compilation of their words on the subject of fathers.

As you read this book, it might be interesting for you to think about how, perhaps, your son or daughter would answer my challenging question of How My Father Influenced My View of What a Man Is. Would you be saddened, delighted, surprised, or appalled by your son or daughter's response to my question? There is a section at the conclusion of this book where you can begin to pursue some of the questions I raise, including the question of how your own father has influenced your view of a man.

One of the themes that will become evident as you read this book is that for most (if not all) families, there are family secrets. They exist because they fulfill a need—a need to cover up shame, a need to protect loved ones from reality, and sometimes a simple need for privacy. Without contemplation and explanation, these secrets fester and too often result in children taking on feelings of guilt or shame.

I recently ran into a former student from twenty years ago. He is now a father, and as we spoke I told him about this book. He commented that he is "pretty harsh" with his son, because, as he tells his wife, "If I am not around, someone has to tell him these things." She has expressed concern to him that their son is not ready to understand many of the messages he is trying to get across. He indicated that their friends, too, think he is hard on the boy, but he is firmly convinced that the way he is raising his child is the right way. When I told him the title of this book and where it comes from, he got a huge grin on his face. He smiled and said, "Done that," and then proceeded to tell the story of how he had put the shaving cream on his face and on his son's; how he had put a cap over the razor, but showed his son how to go against the grain to get a closer shave. He was so proud of having already done this, and the smile was infectious as he spoke about this experience. It was an interesting exchange.

He then told me that a trusted colleague had asked him recently if he had ever shot anyone while he was in the Army. He had never told anyone, including his wife, that he had in fact shot and killed someone. As he told me about this event and expressed his confusion about why he had chosen to respond truthfully for the first time with this colleague, his eyes filled with tears. He said that he doesn't feel guilt or shame over what he did, and he finds that fact disturbing. He fears that others will judge him because he does not feel those things. He did what he had to do, as the other man would have shot him had he not shot first. He even tried to save the man's life after shooting him. Today, twenty-two years later, he is still troubled. He is a husband, yet has never told his life partner about this. He has a young son, and he doesn't want his son to know, either. His own construction of what a man is includes that a man must keep secrets. While he had not thought much about this incident over the past two decades, now that he had spoken about it, he found himself thinking more and more about his closely held secret. When I told this former student that I wanted to include his story in my book, his comment was that, if someone could learn from him, then it would be fine for me to share his experience.

When we keep those family secrets, we pay a pretty high price. I find that fathers want to share their secrets with someone. These secrets are not limited to past actions. Family secrets can, and often do, include keeping our emotions private. Albert's story sets a stage for what I mean and for what will come up again and again in this book.

▶ **Albert**

Several years ago, Albert, a young man I was working with in counseling, talked about his father and his worries about his father's health. His dad was not taking good care of himself, and he was worried about him. I asked Albert if he had told his father about his concerns, and he responded, "We don't talk about things like that." As we pursued this line of discussion, I asked him if he had ever told his dad that he loved him. He replied that he hadn't. When I asked him why, he once again said, "We don't do that in my family." I then asked a question that was to become one of my "stock-in-trade" questions as a counselor: "If Jane (my administrative assistant) knocked on the door and asked to see me, and upon my return I told you that we had just learned that your dad had died, what would you have wished that you had said to him?" Immediately, with no hesitation, he simply said that he would wish that he had told him that he loved him. I handed him the phone and offered to leave the room, but he wasn't ready for that yet—it took him another month and a half before he did talk with his dad and tell him he loved him.

There was never a question about the love between Albert and his dad, but the expression of that love is simply something that too many families "don't do." When I asked Albert why he was able to tell me—almost a complete stranger—that he loved his father but couldn't tell his own dad, he had no answer. This is not an unusual response. Until someone asks us about our emotions, we often keep them so far inside that we don't readily have access to them.

Why does this happen in so many homes and families and relationships? Do you "talk about things like that" in your family? If not—why not? What could the long-term consequences be if you "don't do that?" If you suddenly found out that your father, or mother, or child had died, what would you wish you had said? Sadly, today's most recent tragedies remind us how our lives can change in an instant. If your response is the same as Albert's, what is preventing you from saying that now? Isn't it better to say, "I'm glad I did" rather than, "I wish I had?"

I am intrigued as I watch the men and women search and reflect to try to answer these questions. I recently ran into a colleague at the grocery store, and as we chatted in the food aisle, I told him of the essays I ask students to write on the question of How My Father Influenced My View of What a Man Is. When I mentioned the topic, my colleague stepped back from me and replied, with a grimace, "Not very well." He clearly had a visibly powerful reaction to the mere mention of the topic. He told me that he would be very interested to read my book when it was finished, as he has two sons and is curious about other sons' reactions to their relationships with their fathers.

I have attempted here to gather some of the more interesting reflections from my students, along with my own experiential observations from the interactions I've had with literally thousands of young people over my more than forty years of counseling and teaching. I promised my students that I would protect their anonymity, so I have randomly assigned names to their stories. There will be commentary and some theory, but mostly this book aims to be just the honest and real and sometimes raw reactions of today's college students regarding their relationships—or lack thereof—with their fathers. Of course, not all fathers are of a biological nature, and there will be some discussion in the pages to come about the realities of all kinds of father relationships: the bonds with fathers of friends, the experience of having two fathers, the process of adopting father figures, and more.

This is not a book on how to be a good or better dad. It is a book that asks the simple question of how fathers influence our views of manhood. I will be presenting a variety of student essays, some from men and some from women. At the end of my class, students often tell me that this particular essay affected them more than almost anything else we did throughout the semester—in some cases, in their entire college education. I challenge them to share their papers with their fathers and have had the amazing opportunity to then meet many of those fathers at Commencement. Our discussions are fascinating; the fathers express gratitude and surprise at the papers that their sons and daughters shared. You will see from some of the essays that some students will most likely not be able to share their papers with their fathers. Those students have told me how much this project helped them put some things into perspective.

In my forty-five-plus years of working in education, I have seldom run into fathers who are bad people. I think most fathers are a mystery to their sons and daughters. They haven't always done the best things or what their son or daughter wanted or needed, but in most cases, they have done the best job they knew how to do. I hope this book will provide some insight into how young people today view their fathers (and in several cases, their mothers), and I hope we can all learn from their willingness to share.

Chapter 1

Masculinity and Fathers

Do today's fathers feel that they have to shape themselves to fit stereotypical images of masculinity to be a good parent and role model? Do sons and daughters allow their fathers to be fully human and unique, or are the stereotypical images of fathers, such as are portrayed in the media—television, magazines, and the movies—generationally imprinted? Do sons and daughters expect flawless behavior—a *Father Knows Best* kind of dad, or perhaps a Bill Cosby portraying Dr. Cliff Huxtable? Do fathers need to know best and have all of the answers? Fathers often work terribly hard at being the type of father they believe society expects them to be, and wittingly or unwittingly, many fathers take on the behaviors, attitudes, and morality that surrounded them as they were growing up.

In some of my students' essays addressing How My Father Influenced My View of What a Man Is, many share how grateful they are to their fathers for constructing their view of manhood through a loving and positive example. Others note how they value the lessons learned when they have compared themselves to their friends' fathers. And unfortunately, other students describe more tyrannical fathers who, although often unaware, hurt their children and inflict real emotional pain and psychological damage. It is likely that they are parenting as they were parented and don't know how to do it differently.

When fathers exhibit behaviors and attitudes that fit within society's expectations of a man and father, both sons and daughters learn by example how they, in turn, are supposed to behave as a father, or a son, or a daughter, or a mother. Sadly, limiting and harmful stereotypes of masculinity still influence many of today's youth. These distorted images are often neither accurate nor inclusive portrayals, but if it is all you know, you carry such expectations of men and fathers forward. The social construct of fatherhood, like masculinity, appears to be cyclical and generational.

A lack of communication between men compounds this situation further. Men want to be authentic and honest, but as a society we seldom provide men with a safe environment where candid conversations can occur to explore the real issues confronting men today—expressly, their fears, longings, and insecurities. Additionally, not having real opportunities to talk about the different possible expressions of masculinity leaves young men to rely solely on their observations of the world around them to deduce society's expectations. As a result, many young men buy into harmful images of masculinity because they have not experienced anything different at home, and consequently, distorted images of men endure. I know that these strict and limiting views of masculinity are still going strong in 2013 because of what my students continue to tell me: real men don't cry, feel lost, indecisive, or afraid; real men do like to play or talk about sports; real men take foolish risks and put themselves in danger (You Only Live Once—YOLO); real men are the primary breadwinners; and so on.

***

A consequence of having a distorted image of what a father actually is can— and too often does—cause pain. But it also provides the holder with a measure of all men, and this has serious consequences, as Beth shows us. Her essay reveals how social constructs of gender roles can become generational: She saw what her father did and then generalized his behavior to all males. She also saw her mom's role and generalized her actions to all females, including herself. While Beth recognized that she puts "a significant amount of pressure on the male gender," she still does it and this influences her relationships with men.

▶ **Beth**

"My dad was the first man I ever really knew. Consequently, as a child, I interpreted his unique personality to be one that is able to be generalized to all men. Even today, I find that I continue to use my dad as some sort of measuring stick by which to gauge other males.

Growing up with an unfortunate home life, my dad had to fight for everything. His deceased parents didn't exactly provide much support and his older siblings were already married and enjoying their own children. My dad, who lived with a distant aunt, chose to work hard at school and make something of himself. He still boasts about being Student of the Month in high school and graduating from Ohio State at the very top of his class. Because nothing was ever given to my dad for free, he learned how to be independent and take care of himself. I notice that I am drawn to men now who have these same qualities. I never realized this connection before, but I do feel that men should be strong and independent. I find that I admire men more when they have to work hard and are successful, which unfortunately means that I am putting a significant amount of pressure on the male gender.

As a lawyer, my dad put in a respectable forty hours a week and brought home an impressive paycheck to show for it during my childhood. He worked five days a week, eight to four, every week for as long as I can remember. When he was working, my dad came home every day to a clean house and a well-balanced dinner on the table: stereotypical gender roles in all their glory. When I was younger, it seemed natural for me to make the assumption that females must be submissive and wrap their lives around their husbands. My dad made the money, and whether or not it was fair, that meant he didn't have to take care of home matters.

When I was in high school, my dad went through a series of stressful incidents. He was hospitalized for many months in hopes of fixing his a-fib heart. At this point, he lost his sense of independence and control, which is still something that affects him today. Currently, he is on a spectrum of drugs that unfortunately and inescapably have their fair share of side effects. Lately, he has become especially moody, depressed, and irritated. Unfortunately, he has lost what I think is a passion for life and this has greatly affected my family.

Concurrent with this, my dad was also battling at work, trying desperately to keep his job. He had made a request for some special equipment because of his vision disability, which was denied. Instead of accepting his request, he was told he was going to be laid off for being unable to work. Since my dad thought it was wrong to be fired for having poor vision, he chose to fight it out in court. While this was highly stressful for my dad, I couldn't help but feel proud of him. This complements my assumption that men should be tough and fight for what they want and deserve, as it is their supposed duty to be able to take care of and provide for the family. It's almost like he was back in the fifth grade and the bullies on the playground were calling him four-eyes, and he was standing up for himself. My dad never went back to work there—and I'm not sure he would have wanted to after all that—but he does still get a regular check of compensation in the mail for his disability.

My dad lost more than just a job though; he lost who he was. All his life, my dad had learned that hard work pays off and is rewarding. However, without a job, my dad feels pretty worthless, and I can tell that the lack of daily challenges and achievements have affected who he thinks he is. It's like he doesn't know who he is anymore and that makes it even harder for me to understand his role as a male as well. In other words, my dad had mastered the stereotypical male gender role of being successful at work and supporting the family. When this was taken from him, it's like he no longer was happy with life because he could no longer fill that role.

It is especially confusing because my mom got a job to help support our family monetarily (and also now finally has the freedom to do so as she doesn't have to support my dad's career), yet she still does all the housework. I'm not sure he purposely chooses to refuse to do housework/chores because I don't think he thinks he is above it; however, I do think that because this aspect of his life has always been taken care of for him, he is conditioned not to do it. This leaves my dad with very little to do to help contribute to and support our family. It's like the role of provider has been taken from him, and I can see how it has affected him negatively. His idea of a male is someone who is powerful, in control, and independent. My mom has since taken on these qualities and has also kept her stereotypical female gender role as well. It's as if my dad needs to be that stereotypical male, which makes me feel like all men need to be stereotypically male. I know what happens when males cannot live up to the expectations demanded by society for our gender roles. It's because it is all my dad has ever known and to change so radically at his age seems way too overwhelming for my dad.

I've always assumed that gender roles were purely socially constructed. I thought that perhaps I made assumptions about the male gender because of what I've seen on TV or from other media sources. However, now that I have reflected more specifically on my dad, I can see that I base a lot of my assumptions about men on him. It seems so obvious now that he would be the single one person who defined "what is a man," but growing up, I never thought about it. While it may be difficult for my dad to understand his need to fit into a male gender role, I want to be more optimistic as I understand that I can make my own conclusions."

***

I suspect that most fathers, and not a few mothers, forget that children don't miss much. Think of a young child blurting out a profanity (usually in front of company) that he or she doesn't understand but somehow picked up from being around adults . . . if only all situations were that simple to brush aside. Sometimes, off-hand negative comments from fathers not only sting in the moment but stay with us for a lifetime. Tim's essay strikes me as a fascinating example of just how fathers teach their sons and how high the stakes really are regarding a child's ability to observe. Tim writes, "I remember growing up watching every move my dad made. It was as if I was taking notes for when I got older."

▶ Tim

"When people ask me what I think a 'man' really is and what characteristics it takes to be considered one, I really have trouble answering the question. Often I feel the answer is so obvious that I don't even have to respond. In class, we went around and asked each person in our groups what they thought it meant to be considered a man, and almost all the guys had nothing to say. They were either too afraid to give their real answer or just didn't really have one.

Our culture has so many stereotypes concerning what it takes to be a 'real man,' and I honestly feel that people are brought up differently and have their own definitions. Some boys are raised in a strict environment, almost treated as if they are in the military. Others are raised the total opposite. A lot of families want their boys to grow up and be just like their fathers and carry on a sort of tradition or continue the family legacy. There are a lot of kids I know who were constantly worn down by their fathers to be something that they weren't. I always felt bad for those boys. What kind of life is that for a kid when he is always being heckled about everything and left without the enjoyment of a childhood? Our society feels that men need to be strong, rugged, tough, and athletic. A true man shows no emotion and holds everything in or else he will be considered weak or girly. Men feel that in order to be a man you must obtain these ridiculous qualities or else you'll be considered a failure. I considered myself very lucky growing up and always wondered why my father was so different from some of my friends' fathers.

I was taught about being a man differently. I was an only child and fighting with a brother wasn't an option for me. I was very attached to my parents, and I went pretty much everywhere with them. I couldn't leave their sight. My father didn't treat me like his little soldier, and he never called me "champ" or "his little winner." All he cared about was that I would grow up someday and be able to support a family of my own. Being a 'man' is being able to support those you love, such as your wife and kids. My dad told me that once you start a family, you put everything you have into it, making sure everyone is comfortable and happy. My father is a family man, and does all he can to support my mother and me. Nothing else really matters to him.

Crying and showing emotion were never a sign of weakness in my family; it was just a way of letting my feelings out and expressing them to someone. My father never told me that showing emotion or expressing my feelings was bad; he let me know that it wasn't good to hold things in. He was always looking for what was best for me, not what he wanted me to do.

Fathers are the main focus for little kids—dads have to be aware that every little thing they do is being watched. I remember growing up watching every move my dad made. It was as if I was taking notes for when I got older. It wasn't that I wanted to be a doctor and make lots of money, but I wanted to have the same qualities he had and present myself the same. I have learned from my father that to be considered a man you need to be able to look at yourself in the mirror every morning and be proud of who you are. I am proud of the man I am becoming and I owe it all to my father. He goes against every stereotypical word used to describe 'a real man' today. I believe that if you work hard, sacrifice, and give everything you have to those you love, you are considered a man. It doesn't take a rough and tough guy to be a man—it's how you show love and support for loved ones around you, and the extra mile you go for them, that makes you one. My father was the biggest influence on me when it came to becoming that kind of man."

***

The role that mothers play in compensating for certain fathers fascinates me. Some of my students never realized (until this assignment), just how much their mothers compensated for their dads' physical or emotional absence. When my students recognize the value of their mothers through their understanding of men's roles, they are sometimes surprised and sometimes saddened—saddened that their mothers often taught them more about what being a man is than their fathers did. They are also taken aback when I ask if they have ever told their mothers how much they are appreciated—most never have.

Wendy stopped by recently to give me the permission form that is required for me to include student essays in this book. I had not seen her in a while, and she is now married with a child of her own. Sometimes, when my students have their own children, they report that their own fathers finally have come to understand their "errors." The elder parent realizes or admits that they may not have always done the best job, or the job that their own son or daughter needed. The new common bond—the grandchild—is often what prompts these fathers to change, and this can provide a second chance. In Wendy's case, it didn't. With tears in her eyes, she told me, "He hasn't changed, Dave. Not a bit. I worry how it will affect my being a mom, and how it will impact my relationship with my husband."

▶ Wendy

"What is a man? How has my father socially constructed my vision of a man? I am required to write a response to this question, but I ponder for hours as I struggle to find the definition of a man that I have been raised to believe. I start by looking online. What is the Webster's definition? My results were very broad. Everything defined a man as a human, or a distinct race of human. As I continued to read I stumbled onto one particular definition. A man 'is the sole living representative of the hominid family.' Socially, I have been taught that the man was the 'sole representative.' However, I was not raised by my father alone but also by my mother. The two of them held a partnership. My mother was a very strong—some might say hardheaded—woman. She believed in freedom of speech and that a woman's place was the same as a man's. She constantly represented that she was not dependent on my father, and they equally shared all household responsibilities. They cooked, cleaned, plowed the driveway, and took care of us kids together. My father did not form my social construction of a man alone; he did it with the equal help of my mother.

My parents had very equal roles in our family and I believe that played a large part in the way I constructed manhood. You often hear of the woman staying at home to raise the children, cook, and clean, while the husband is away at work. In my family, both of my parents worked. My mother would get us up and ready for daycare or school in the morning, and my father would pick us up after work and make dinner for the family. My father and mother worked equally on all household responsibilities. This was very different than what was done in the past. This made me believe that men and women were equal and capable of conducting the same responsibilities. My mother and father both coached my softball and my brother's baseball teams. This was another form of equal responsibilities. When it came down to physical abilities, my father and mother showed me that a man is just as capable as a woman.

When it came to my parents' hobbies, they often varied. My father enjoyed outdoor 'manly activities' while my mother enjoyed 'feminine things.' Manly activities in our household consisted of hunting and fishing. These activities made up my father's most precious enjoyments. Growing up, if I wanted to do something with my father, those were the activities. He bought me a rifle when I was eight so I could go hunting with him. We would also go fishing. In the wintertime, it was a treat to go out ice fishing with my dad. During all of these activities, my mother would stay home and clean or go and do activities that she enjoyed. I don't know what made these activities seem so masculine to me. For decades the man has been the hunter for the family. I always participated in these activities as a way to spend time with my father. To this day I would not turn to my girlfriends and ask them to go ice fishing with me. They would be grossed out and ask if I was crazy. Going with a man made me feel comforted and taken care of. When I go hunting or ice fishing with any male, I always expect that he must know what he is doing because he is a male. And that I must be safe because he has to have done this a thousand times—because this is what males do. But when I talk to a male and tell them I love to hunt and fish, they look at me like I am ridiculous. Why would a girl enjoy these activities? They seem to think I should be shopping and not enjoying the great outdoors, and I am definitely in trouble if I hold a greater knowledge of any of these outdoor activities than the male might have. Some men might not be repelled by my knowledge, but as a girl when I represent my knowledge, I am immediately looked at as a friend and not as a cute, datable girl.

When I look at my parents from an emotional perspective, I can see a large difference. Although physically they seem to be the same, emotionally they are very different. My mother is very open and talks everything out with us. My father was the final disciplinarian and not so verbal. I could always fight with my mother, but my father always ended those fights. When he walked into the room we knew the argument was done. He held the stiff hand and was not afraid to use it. My mother ran the house; my father made sure it stayed that way. That is my image of a 'man of the house': someone who will work equally to keep the family together, but who will always have the final word on how things occur. My mother was the one who would talk us through things if we had a problem. My father was there to do activities with. My brother and I both agree we would never go to my father to discuss a personal problem, or how our day was, or how we were feeling. My father never showed emotion.

I recall the first time my father ever spoke to me with a little emotion. It was just last year, when we were sitting in the hunting blind together, waiting quietly for a big buck to walk out. As I mentioned before, hunting gives me time to spend with my father, and so I go every chance I get. While we were sitting quietly, Dad said, "Tomorrow would be Papa's seventieth birthday." My grandfather had died that year, and his absence was still hard on all of us. I sat there, not knowing what to say. We never discuss emotions or personal things together. I stared ahead, trying not to cry and wishing I knew how to respond. If this conversation were with my mother, I could have told her that I missed my Papa, and asked her how to deal with the loss. But with my father, I just sat there, because you don't discuss those things with a man. A man does not discuss emotions. What you see is what you get.

Today, as I am graduating college and have not lived at home in over two years, the relationship with my father is distant. What relationship we do have is through my mother, who will tell me things like, "Your father called you three days ago. Why haven't you called him back? He is upset," or "Your father was angry that you didn't say good-bye to him when you left the other day." This shows me that men do have emotions that they keep in, and I sometimes wonder if this just means they have a harder time expressing them. I wonder if, unlike the way women seem to do, men don't analyze every situation. When they say something, that is what they mean. They don't say something with the hopes that someone will notice that they are implying something else."

***

When we learn that someone is expecting a child, how many of us ask, "Are you hoping for a boy or a girl?" With today's technology, prospective parents are able to find out the sex of a developing fetus if they so desire. The nursery then gets decorated to fit the sex of the new baby—blue for boys and pink for girls. (Visit any toy store and see just how strongly we are conditioned to color code in this way.) Some expectant fathers, when they find that they are going to have a son, rush out to buy small footballs or baseball gloves. What happens when a father who wants a son has a daughter? Even though Valerie counters her father's comments about her not being a son with humor and understanding, she still remembers those comments. How did this affect her actions as she tried to fit in as "one of the boys," instead of simply being who she is?

▶ **Valerie**

"Growing up, the ongoing joke between my father and me was that he threw away a baseball glove when I was born, in disappointment that I was not a boy. I always knew that he was only kidding, and that he loved and cherished his two daughters more than anything in the world. He has always been supportive of whatever we wanted to pursue, and yes, playing softball was on the list. My father has played an incredibly strong and very important role in my life; he has also constructed my views of what a man is supposed to be like.

My dad has been a police officer for twenty-nine years. I think most children think that police officers can do many things and have many answers. My dad certainly seemed to have many answers, including some I did not want to hear. For much of my life, my father worked a rotating schedule. He was away from home working many nights. I always felt a sense of sadness when he was working the night shift because he was not with us. But I knew that because of the job he did my mother could work part-time, and for many years she worked in the same school that my sister and I attended.

I consider my father to be a handyman, who at times can be rather stubborn and not admit that he could use a helping hand. I have also seen my grandfather time and time again refuse to ask for help, especially with large projects. I have witnessed my dad argue with his father about not asking for help and not realize that he is a mirror image of Grandpa. I guess the apple really does not fall far from the tree—I know from whom I get my stubborn streak. Much of what I have learned from my father has come from watching the example he sets. My dad followed the examples of his father, so it makes sense that my dad taught me some of the same. Although I am not a male, some character traits such as honesty and hard work have no gender correlation. Some do.

Although my dad does not like to ask for help, he is quick to help others. I believe being independent is the main component of the male image. I think most males take pride in providing for themselves and for their family without help from others. When help is needed there seems to be a bit of unofficial bartering that takes place: "one hand washes the other." My dad is much more likely to accept help if he can give something back. In this regard, I believe my dad has taught me that we should not look to "take a free ride." He is a very hard worker and very honest. He has told me many times that if something is not worth working for it is not worth having, this would even include my grades at school. My dad has set a very high priority on education. His sense of persistence and dedication to a task has been an inspiration to me in overcoming my learning difference.

I really think that my dad dreamed of having a son. I often stepped in and pretended to fill that role. Many of my vivid memories from growing up revolve around the usage of our family boat. During the summer, I would get up at 6 am and go fishing with my Papa, Dad, and two cousins (both boys). At the time I felt like 'one of the boys,' and I was often treated like one as well. My dad and my cousins would poke fun at me when I could not catch a fish or bait the worm correctly. Although I was the target of their jokes, they all made sure I was having fun. One by one they would hook a fish and pretend it got away, then moments later they would ask me to hold their pole while they opened a soda or washed their hands. Of course, I would reel the fish in while acting very excited. My dad started this tactic, and it was quickly picked up by the boys. Making sure the ladies have fun is a male priority.

One of the most important things my father taught me was to stand up for myself. He always said, "Don't start crap . . . and don't take it!" Starting when we were very young, my father would wrestle with my sister and me. I think he was exposing us to some sort of self-defense. I remember the day when my parents returned home from a parent-teacher conference with some very strict instructions for me: "Leave the boys alone." I guess I was a bit aggressive on the playground; the boys wanted to play two-hand touch and I thought the only way to play football was to tackle. I think my dad was proud, but my mom was not.

To this day, I refer back to what my father taught me. Although these are images of what a male should be, they have come in very handy in my everyday life. My dad has influenced and guided me by what he has said, but most important, by what he has done. Actions certainly speak louder than words."

***

Earlier, I mentioned the power of the word disappoint when applied by a parent to a child. John shows us some of this power, which, in his case, was also accompanied by his understanding of right and wrong. Through John's story, we see how the passage of time cannot dull the lessons we learn from our fathers—even the good ones.

▶ John

"In my first year at Saint Michael's College, I took the first-year seminar entitled, The Examined Life. This course was dedicated to reading memoirs, and each student produced his or her own memoir at the culmination of the semester. I wrote about my father. I find it very funny that I am sitting here three years later doing that same exact thing. My story was entitled, 'My Father and Me: From Trees to Truth.' It focused on my relationship with him over the years, and the lessons that I have learned under his guidance, wisdom, and aegis. I told many stories about good times that my father and I have had together, but I focused more on the areas where I was slipping. It was in these areas that my father showed me what it means to not just be a man but also a person.

In seventh grade, I was terrified that my parents would see that I was not faring so well on my progress reports—I had a couple of C's and incompletes in a couple of classes. In an effort to hide this from my parents I forged my dad's signature on the progress reports, and I told my parents that the teachers were not sending anything home for the students who were doing well in their classes. In my head it was a foolproof plan, but my dad is a much smarter man than I am. He is a dentist in the area so a lot of my classmates' parents see him at one time or another during the year. Needless to say, he found out fairly quickly that I was attempting to pull the wool over his eyes. When he finally found out that I had forged his signature he was none too pleased with me. Early one morning he made me go into the school and apologize to each one of my teachers and discuss my grades in each class with them. Almost ten years have gone by since then, and I still feel like an idiot for doing that. Now I can laugh about the stupidity of my actions, but then I felt like such a dope. I had not angered my dad but made him disappointed.

My dad didn't take the time to explain to me why what I had done was wrong because I knew what I did was wrong to begin with. It was my error and my poor decision making that led to the mistake. My father didn't need to point that out to me. What my father did do was to explain to me that he will always be there for me no matter what I do, and many kids are not as lucky to have a father who loves me like he does. I think this statement has been true throughout my entire life. Despite all the times I have lied to my parents and been caught, and the times that I haven't been caught, my dad has shown that he has an unconditional love for me. Not just for me, but for all of my family members. We have definitely been pains in his ass throughout our childhood, adolescence, and rise into adulthood, but he has shown us how understanding, caring, and fair he is with all of us. Stubborn as we all can be, my dad has shown me what patience is and the importance of loving the people around you."

***

Les learns a difficult and interesting lesson early on about love and fear. As awareness of child abuse issues increases, the use of physical force by fathers is changing. For Les, his father's use of physical force to enforce rules or to remind him of who was in control has left its mark. For better or worse, Les has been able to put the memories into a wider context to reach understanding and appreciation for his father.

▶ Les

"I have been socialized to become a 'man' since the day of my birth. Becoming a 'man' has been my calling. Coming out the womb, I was a young, impressionable, naïve individual with no initial concept of the most ubiquitous categorizing characteristic of human beings: gender.

However, unbeknownst to me, I was already on the path to manhood—in some respects, my path was predetermined. Of those who kept me on this path, the single most powerful socializing agent was my father. Throughout my childhood, adolescence, and later 'emerging adulthood,' my father has molded my masculinity through numerous implicit and explicit ways.

When I was a young child, I was aggressive toward my sister. I used to hit her, tease her, and generally just be a nuisance. Quite frankly, I'm surprised she still loves me at all. My aggression toward my sister let me take a glimpse into how fathers and mothers differ. When I hurt my sister around my mother, I was quickly reprimanded verbally. I would get a: 'Leave your sister alone!' One phrase in particular would consistently strike fear into me—the 'Wait until your father gets home!' In some respects, I learned to fear, while also respect and love, my father. This general ambivalence toward my father—this love and fear—seems to be common in father-son relationships.

My father was definitely sterner than my mother in his verbal reprimands and would spank me if I really got on his nerves. I learned what it was to be masculine through these interactions. I learned that a father enforces the rules of the house with the strength of physical force, fear, and intimidation, if they are required. I also quickly came to understand who was the head of our household, who was in control, who was the decision maker: unequivocally, that was the 'man,' the father. In summary, a father has to be in control and use force in order to maintain that control."

***

The quote that Patrick chose to begin his essay with raises many important issues. When we think that our upbringing is difficult or complex or sometimes impossible to comprehend, how often do we project this onto our fathers and wonder if our struggles compare? But how are we supposed to understand what our fathers went through if they never share their experiences with us? My students have often come to understand this weighty generational legacy: their fathers' relationships with their own fathers (grandfather) affected how they raised children.

▶ **Patrick**

" 'I've had a hard life, but my hardships are nothing against the hardships that my father went through in order to get me to where I started.'

— *Bartrand Hubbard*

My father taught me lots of things that I use every day, like how to drive a car or how to tell a maple tree from a spruce. He imparted to me a love of history, and I'm pretty sure I get my thirst for knowledge from him as well, though he has to constrain it often. I learned how to discuss and compromise from him, and his dry sense of humor continues to live on in me (or at least so I've been told). These are the obvious, tangible things that my father passed onto his son. But he's likely passed far more than just these onto me. In fact, I know he has.

In most people's sense of the word, my father had a difficult childhood. In a constant struggle to keep his new company afloat, his father worked grueling hours at his construction company, named after him. My dad spent most of his time outside in the rural town center, playing ball with his friends, without the influence of a father. This absence was devastatingly compounded at age nine when his mother died. He told me privately a few years ago, 'I still don't know how she died.' How do you live with that mystery every day of your life? This understandably destroyed any sense of a normal childhood for my father. It would also have long-lasting repercussions when he himself became a parent. With a mother deceased and a father often gone, he had no real role models to look up to. He had to grow up by himself. He lost himself in sports in high school and entered into the workforce after high school, doing odd jobs like driving a septic truck (my mother has fond memories of him picking her up for a date in the truck once), but eventually ending up in the family company. He was dating my mother by his early twenties and had not elected to attend college. 'In those days, you could do that,' he often tells me. Though this may seem like an idealized portrait (and I guess it is, to a certain extent), he still had many flaws.

I was born one year after my mother and father got married—they were twenty-four years old at my birth. It soon became apparent, and he has told me since: He didn't know how to be a parent. With little parental influence of his own until he began working, he was thrust into a situation that he was utterly unprepared for. He told me stories of, when my mother worked, how he would take me down to my grandmother's (his mother-in-law) house and rock me in a cart with her guiding eye. He didn't trust himself. As I grew, it became obvious that my mother would have a much larger influence on me because my father was always at work. Sometimes he'd be sent away to places like Pennsylvania for a week or two at a time. When he was around the house, we got along fine, but sometimes he could get angry—he had a bit of a temper, and that sort of thing scares a kid.

There was intense pressure on me to do well in school. If I didn't, both parents would get angry with me. They had very high expectations of me. When I disappointed them, I would get a stern lecture, or even be punished (a grounding, or limited privileges). I would be terrified if my grades were below par, and I don't know if it's because he was the man, or he was bigger, or what, but I was the most scared of my father when something went wrong.

I was also pressured into playing sports. This is the way in which my father became a man, and he wanted me to do the same. His actions, to a certain extent, made sense: All around him, parents were letting their kids watch TV all day and not caring if they went outside at all. 'I lived outside,' my father always tells me. Plus, he thought it would be a good way for me to make friends, get exercise, and learn to be part of a team, to work together to overcome something. My outlet was eventually soccer—baseball didn't really suit me.

My dad was the assistant coach. We would practice for hours at the field, him and me: trapping, heading, passing. I was sent to soccer camp. I learned my position like the back of my hand. I was let out of elementary school early a few times to watch the local college compete at their home field. But I never really got excited about it. I tried to stop playing several times. Part of the reason was because I was being forced to play. Another reason was that, if I played badly, I would get a long lecture by an angry father on the way home. I would try to get out of playing, but I was always made to. The big confrontation occurred in my sophomore year of high school. I didn't want to play, and that was that. There was a huge showdown between him and me. It ended badly. He was furious at me and refused to talk to me for several days. That had never happened to me before, and it really shook me.

It took him some time to calm down, but when he did, we had a long conversation and worked things out. I think that, along with the death of his father, this was the start of a transformation for him. His temper began to leave him, and he began to really cherish the time he spent with the family. He continually said to me that his biggest regret in life was that he didn't spend more time with his kids. But he knew that through his hard work, he was able to guarantee that my sister and I were able to go to college. His former tendency to demand and intimidate was replaced by trust in my decisions and belief that I could choose for myself. The last few years have really had him become very supportive of me in all aspects."

***

I have read over 300 student essays on the topic of the students' fathers. This one, in particular, has had a powerful impact on me. Geri is bright, responsible, and a good, effective student leader. She is someone who will be an amazing professional in the field of counseling or social services, but she has never understood or accepted her own skills and gifts. This essay reveals why. As I mentioned in the introduction to this chapter, society's expectations for masculinity can sometimes affect fatherhood in harmful ways; Geri's story is a poignant illustration.

▶ Geri

"When I was a kid, everyone thought I was a 'daddy's girl' because I spent so much time with my father. It's true, I did spend quite a lot of time with my dad, but only out of necessity; he needed the help, and my mom was emotionally unable to care for me. As a girl, I learned a great deal about men from him, or rather what he thought it meant to be a man. I have since been let down by my father so many times, I dare not try to count. I have come to know that much of my education was wrong, but there are still some feelings I have toward men that I can't get rid of. The lessons my father taught me have left scars so deep, I fear they now keep me from making meaningful, lasting relationships with males, save the few I currently have— no thanks to my dad.

Lesson number one: Men are obsessed with what you look like, and something can always be improved about your appearance. These standards are often unattainable, which is why you should constantly be watching yourself and your physical appearance, often to the detriment of your health.

I was a tomboy-type girl most of my life. In high school, I wore mostly black, baggy clothes and dyed my hair all sorts of crazy colors—a full head of green hair was my favorite. On top of this, I have always been on the heavy side, constantly fighting my love for food. These things were never acceptable. My father tried to buy me dresses, told me at least once a week that I needed to exercise and join a sport at school, and said that crazy hair made me look stupid. 'Don't you want people to think you're pretty?' he would ask.

As I got older, I started to notice that my mom seemed to be having a lot of back problems. When I asked her to consider getting a breast reduction to reduce the strain and ease the pain of her permanent bra strap marks, her reply disturbed me. In the state of Virginia, a tubal ligation needs to be approved by the husband—my father refused to let her get a tubal ligation, so she never even asked him about the breast reduction surgery because he always told her that he likes her size 44F breasts. Like me, she has also always had a problem with her weight, and my dad makes sure to let both her and I know that we are not up to par. Every meal, every snack, every drink is monitored and comes with a comment; he will kindly suggest in a condescending tone that what you have is 'no good for you, you know,' while finishing off his pint of Ben & Jerry's Chubby Hubby.

This lesson has taught me that my body and appearance are unacceptable in the eyes of men, and that every guy I pass is judging me, what I'm wearing, and what I'm eating. In order to be appealing to men, I need to sacrifice because guys won't like me if I'm ugly and fat.

Lesson number two: A man is the head of the house. Men work harder than their wives, and the house belongs to them. Men don't cook or do housework, and they deserve their own space in the house, away from family and the wife.

I can't remember a time when my dad did the dishes, or even put his dishes in the dishwasher for that matter. I can, however, remember countless times when he got up from the living room, walked through the kitchen, and interrupted me doing my homework to tell me that I needed to do the dishes; he would promptly walk back to watch TV. When my mom and I go somewhere by ourselves (it could be a day, it could be a week), we come home and the dishes are in the sink, the bed is unmade, there's laundry stacked up in my parents' bedroom, and he asks us what's for dinner.

My father also reminds us that the house is his and his alone, despite the fact that my mother earns about the same as him. Whenever I want to have friends over, it must be approved in advance, on his time, and they must leave when he gets tired of people. But when he wants people over, my mom and I are lucky if we get a day's notice to prepare a meal and clean the house for a party of ten or twenty people. My dad also has the majority of the basement designated as his space for his things, including a pool table, air hockey table, table saw, and his Redskins-themed movie room. Oh, and the whole two-car garage is filled with his tools, as is the shed out back. When my friends come over, he complains that he has nowhere to go.

This lesson has taught me that my lot in life is to be the servant housewife; regardless of my career goals and salary, I will never truly be the owner of my home. My husband gets to decide what and when things happen, and he will require a variety of spaces to get away from me. My money means nothing, and my worth is based solely on my cleaning habits, recipe book, and the aforementioned obsession with how I look.

Lesson number three: Men truly only care about other men and their mothers. Fathers only want sons. Wives and daughters are side notes, often they just get in the way.

My mom and I have always been second to my father's mom—my grandmother. She says jump, Dad asks how high. But if my mom and I need something, we have to wait. My father pays her phone and cable bill and fixes her car for free; he reshingled her roof, built her a game room, and paid for all the supplies. When my mom bought herself a new sewing machine because her twenty-year-old one broke, he told her she was being frivolous and spending too much money. He demands breakfast for Father's Day but spends the rest of the day at his mother's house—then yells at me for having my boyfriend over while he's gone.

Trying to speak to my dad is next to impossible because he thinks he's always right, and when you can actually get a conversation started, he often doesn't actually pay attention to you. My mother has been fighting with the TV for my dad's attention since they got married, and it is no different with me. When the TV is on, he couldn't be less interested in what I have to say. My mom told me once that she stood in front of the TV naked to try to get his attention; he asked her to move because she was blocking the game.

My father has also made it abundantly clear that I am his biggest disappointment. As his only child, I had to play the role that my nonexistent brother would have played as well as being the daughter. I had to haul wood, clean cars, and play ball with my dad, but I also had to be pretty and wear dresses and do laundry. I am neither the strong, athletic, car-enthusiast son nor the pretty, thin, princess–daddy's girl daughter. And as such, the few things I am good at are not enough. My grades are good, but they're not high enough; I got into a good school, but it's not in-state; I finally got a boyfriend (so at least I'm not a lesbian), but he's a no-good loser.

This lesson is probably the most painful one. Apparently, I will only deserve a roof over my head after my future husband has taken care of his mother, and even then, she will come first. What I think will never be as important as a man's opinion, and what I have to say will always be trumped by the television. This has taught me that I, by my sheer existence, am inadequate.

Lesson number four: Men do physical labor, and men work on cars. If a male can't do physical labor, he's not a man. You can always tell how a man will treat you by how he takes care of his vehicle.

My father made sure to tell me all of his own childhood strife. He had to help his parents build their house; he didn't have friends because he had to take care of his siblings; he had to build his first car; he had to work to help with the bills. And today, he refuses to hire people to do work for him—from plumbing to room-building to working on cars, my dad does it all by himself. Asking for help is weak. He told me that being able to do it by yourself shows that you can take care of yourself and your family.

When his sister got engaged, my dad absolutely hated her fiancé because he never offered to help out with the various fix-it problems at my grandparents' house. When he offered to help build my grandparents' game room, my dad suddenly loved him. The same thing happened with my other uncle—a photographer who hires contractors and plumbers. My aunt has been married to the photographer for twenty years, but he only recently offered to help with a random project at my grandparents' house. After two decades of disliking my uncle, my father told me, 'Your uncle has finally earned my respect because he helped build that deck.'

Physical labor is not the only indicator of manliness. An even better indicator is the man's ability to take care of a car. This care goes beyond just changing the oil and a flat tire; how a man takes care of his car shows how he'll take care of his woman. If he has a run-down, old 'beater' vehicle, he obviously doesn't care about women at all, and he will inevitably treat you like garbage—just like he treats his car. My boyfriend's first car was a 1999 Toyota Corolla with two or three different colors, no hubcaps, and dents aplenty. This vehicle was purchased by his parents pre-owned, used by them for a few years, given to his older sister, and then handed down to him when he got his license. My father and grandfather both told me that this Corolla was a sign of things to come, that his piece-of-shit car showed how poorly he was going to treat me. It was a declaration of laziness.

This lesson has taught me that unless a guy takes precious care of his car and does lots of manual labor, he shouldn't be trusted. Other kinds of males are useless, idle, and not actually men at all. A man should be measured by how much labor he does, and he should not be respected unless he shows off his ability to build and fix. These abilities show everyone your worth and that you deserve to be called a man.

I do not believe that my dad is a bad man. I think he tried to do the best he knew how from what his parents taught him. But despite my attempts to please my father, nothing I do ever seems good enough. I wish, just once, that he would tell me he was proud of me without adding a 'but' on the end. I wish that his love didn't come with impossibly tight, unrealistic strings. I wish that when he gave me a gift, it was out of a genuine desire to see a smile on my face—not as an apology for something he did, or as a bribe to get what he wants. More than that, though, I wish that he loved me enough to want me to be happy. It seems I'm not worth the hit his ego takes, and I'm not worth his unconditional love.

All of these lessons, though I know many are false truths, have left an impression on me that I cannot easily shake. I am terrified of most men, and I often do not feel that I am worthy of a man's attention or praise. I can count the number of males in my life on one hand, and they are the only men I trust. What my father didn't teach me is this: I know that men can be kind and honest and caring. I know that they can be artistic and clumsy and absolutely in love with musicals. I know that a man's worth is not measured by his strength, ability, or paycheck. And I know that a man can love somebody unconditionally and with all his heart, regardless of how he takes care of his car."

Chapter 2

Fathers and Tears

When is it all right for a man to cry? How do men learn that it is all right to cry in some situations (funerals, sporting events—an interesting duality), but not in other situations? Socially acceptable behaviors are taught by what we see, or in many cases, by what we hear. *"Don't cry!" "Only girls cry!" "Tears are for babies!" "What are you, a wuss?"* These diminishing expressions have been tossed at and heard by men for ages. But why are men afraid to show their emotions and cry? What labels do we apply to men who do shed tears? Where do we learn to apply these labels so quickly?

A student who was the youngest of twelve children lost his father when he was a senior in high school and his mother when he was a first-year student in college. At their funerals, he recalled to me that he was told by his male siblings not to cry. He never understood why, but he followed their instructions and finds it difficult to cry even today—some twenty years later.

As a society, we ridicule men who cry in public. You only have to look to the current speaker of the House of Representatives in Washington, when John Boehner cries (he does it a lot), he is ridiculed by members of both parties and closely scrutinized by the media. It seems as if every camera in America is trained on him, waiting for the tears to run down his face. Regardless of your political affiliation, a man who cries in public is looked down upon. Crying is seen by too many as a sign of weakness.

Where does all of this come from? Women are allowed and often expected to show sadness and other emotions through tears. Interestly, some men think that women use tears as a strategy to manipulate men—the underlying assumption is that men hate to see women cry. Aren't tears a natural response to an emotional situation? Or is that only true for women?

There is a psychiatric condition known as alexithymia that may help explain the inability of some men to express their emotions—of course, not all men suffer from it. Whether the tendency is genetically based (I will leave that question up to biologists) or it is learned behavior is an interesting question. With the proliferation of mass media, we are now exposed to many different models of men through commercials, movies, television characters, and print media; however, it is difficult *not* to see men portrayed as having limited expressions of emotion. Often in these fictional situations the only emotion expressed by men is anger. All people experience a broad spectrum of emotions, but men in particular don't seem to know that it is all right to express the full range of human emotions in clear and healthy ways.

***

Two female students, Karen and Trish, provide us with a glimpse at how their fathers' expression of emotion has affected them. It seems that witnessing the healthy expression of their fathers' emotion—especially by crying—has had positive repercussions for both women.

▶ Karen

"I have seen my father cry when he's sad, throw a fit when he's angry, and cheer at the television when he's excited. Men *should* show their feelings, just as all people should; otherwise, we are internalizing something that will butt its head in an unwanted place or at an inopportune time. If I had never seen my dad cry, I probably wouldn't accept it as appropriate to see other men cry. My father has always made an effort to communicate his emotions and feelings to my sisters and me, as well as to my mother, and this has dramatically contributed to my thoughts of male communication in relationships."

▶ Trish

"Today, my relationship with my father has made a turnaround from what it was during my high school years. That has a lot to do with the fact that between my junior year of high school and freshman year of college, all of my grandparents—both my maternal and paternal grandparents—passed away. It was during their wakes and funerals that I saw my father cry for the first time, and I think it was the time that he realized that my siblings and I had internalized the stereotype that 'men don't talk about their feelings.' From then on my relationship has grown with my father."

***

The message about masculinity that Isaac internalizes when he thinks he's "supposed to know how" to do something and then can't is a message fraught with both shame and guilt. As mentioned earlier, issues of shame and guilt are not easy for anyone to deal with, much less a young man or woman. We have to wonder what price Isaac pays when he consciously holds his emotions in check. How much energy does he waste in doing this? How does his self-concept deal with the conflict between how he feels and how he expresses those feelings?

▶ **Isaac**

"Looking back on my childhood I can only remember one specific instance where my father told me to change my behavior because it did not represent male characteristics. He very rarely commented on my actions unless they were simply inappropriate or I deserved some type of commendation. I consider myself very lucky to have a father who never passed judgment on the way I liked to act and therefore very rarely critiqued me on my everyday behavior. Although my father's influence over my perception of a man was not directly verbal, I realize now that his actions had a very large effect on how I identify with masculinity.

As a young boy, I always noticed my dad working on different projects around the house; before my father went into the financial services industry, where he works today, he worked as a carpenter for a small and privately owned construction company. Needless to say, these projects often dealt with building something for the house or for the beach to make our lives a little more comfortable or enjoyable. All the work was hands-on and never required hired help; I was convinced that my dad could do it all, and at some points I think he convinced himself, too. This led to some failed ventures, but through failure came learning opportunities that my dad always took full advantage of. Dad would sit at the kitchen table looking over the single sheet of paper he used to plan the job and examine it, sometimes for hours, until he found his flaw. He would then recalculate his numbers until he discovered a way to make it work, or he would start from scratch and try a different approach. He would then grab his tool belt, go back out into the garage and find a way to make his plan work, even if it required some improvisational changes.

Reflecting on my life up to this point, I realize that this process has had a profound effect on how I view masculinity and manhood. I've discovered that my perception of masculinity has a large correlation with independence. I noticed that Dad never asked for help; the only help he would ask for was with the physical labor if it required more than two hands. In that instance, he would get my brothers and me to help. However, when it came to preparation, planning, and assembly, he never felt like he needed to ask for help, usually because he did not need it.

When analyzing how my perception of masculinity was influenced by these actions, I notice that I associate 'masculine work' with fields like carpentry and I often get mad at myself because I am not a good builder like my father. I catch myself wishing that I knew how to work a skill saw or knew how to build the rink we put up every year; I ask myself why I never learned that stuff and I say, 'You're supposed to know how to do that stuff, that's what men do, that's what dad does.' I actually feel a little ashamed that I never took a major interest in learning that stuff as a kid. Dad never shied away from gritty jobs. If he had the skill set and knowledge to do it, he never hesitated to complete it himself. To me, this inferred that men must always be willing to embrace dirt and sweat in order to finish the necessary task. Dad has always worked hard for our house, and he has never been one to concede to a chore unless he knows he lacks the expertise to do it.

One thing I've noticed about Dad that truly resonates with me is his composure. Dad is always even-keeled when it comes to housework; my perception of men with regard to this revolves around the idea that work needs to get done so men do the work, plain and simple. I learned from my dad that men do not complain, because it just makes the work more frustrating to do. Embrace the job and try to enjoy the small things about your task. My dad taught me through his housework that men do not complain and they do not need the gratification of others to feel good about the work they just finished. Because either way, the job had to get done and in those situations men step up and take responsibility to finish the task at hand without letting others know about any burden they may have had to take on.

Emotions present one area where my dad and I differ quite a bit; I very rarely see my dad cry and I have never seen him break down into something even as small as a quiet sob. Dad never told me directly that crying did not coincide with masculinity; however, through his ability to control his emotions and a few recommendations to toughen up when I thought I was hurt, I got the impression that crying was not something boys did. This never stuck with me, though, mainly because I never felt like I could fully control myself; if I felt like I had to cry, I cried, and I accepted that.

These days, interestingly enough, I try to cry less; if I feel the urge approach, I try to suppress it enough where I may tear up but I do not sob. I hold back because I get embarrassed when I am blatantly crying, and my embarrassment definitely has to do with a perception that men do not cry. While my father had a little to do with this, I don't think he had enough of an influence in this area to blame my embarrassment on him. When something upsets me enough to bring me to tears—like a death in the family or a game that turned into a tough emotional loss, I never feel like I have to hold back my emotions. But the one situation that I never let myself break down in is in regard to pain, and this is directly because of my dad. My dad has always stressed the importance of toughness in both sports and in life. As a young kid playing hockey, whenever I started to cry because I got bumped and thought I was hurt, my dad would ask me if I was really hurt or sometimes he would be as ruthless as to ask me if I was dying. When I said no, it always put the pain in perspective for me. I would say to myself, "Yeah, Isaac, you're not really hurt. Get up and stop crying."

***

Zack shares with us the very direct messages he received from his father about not crying. Those early directions can become quite powerful, especially when they are given by the most significant person in a young man's life. Zack, like so many in this class, remembers the interactions word for word. I suspect that his father had no idea how weighty his admonition about crying would be, even years later.

▶ Zack

"For many boys, the first and most influential male in their life is their father, and I am no different. My ideas of what and how a man is supposed to be were constructed almost completely by my father's example. Many aspects of what I do and the ways I act hinge on the ideas that were instilled in me by him—some intentionally, and some not.

When I was young, I was in a bowling league, and for whatever reason, it was an amazingly emotional league to me. I cared more about winning those games than basically anything. After doing well enough to make it into the 'King of the Hill' tournament, which was the biggest bowling event around for my age, I basically told myself that I had to win. In the championship round, after leading by twenty pins, I was robbed (at least in my mind) by the pins, and lost to someone who was definitely a better bowler than I was. At this point, my emotions got the better of me, and I started to cry. Almost instantly, my dad pulled me away from everyone, and not only put the fear of god in me, but made me realize that crying is not allowed in public, for basically any reason. To this day, I have only seen my father cry once, which was at his father's funeral. He also taught me many other things through his actions and words.

A man's father usually gives the basis for how a man thinks a typical man should be and act. In my case, I have learned that men are big and strong, and even when they feel sad, they maintain the curtain of happiness. The way I think a man is supposed to be was influenced greatly by my father's ideas. And from what he has told me in the past, his ideas were based on how he thought his father should be, not how he was. I also know that my father's idea of a man is very outdated, and that there are many different ideas about the way a man should be."

***

The next two stories show us the importance some fathers (and then their sons), place on sports and competition. Phil and Mike provide us with insight into society's valuation of stoicism—even in light of real pain and possible serious injury. The concept is pervasive in today's sports culture and finds its way into the way men deal with nonsports-related interactions, too. In Phil's essay, we see how men often "take care" of others at the expense of their own emotions.

▶ Phil

"Leading by example is a very powerful way to teach. I've never seen my father skip a day of work, smoke a cigarette, or be wasted on booze. I saw him cry once when I was nineteen after our dog drowned in our pool, but he didn't know that I was watching. It was one of the saddest sights of my life; I wanted to comfort him, but I didn't want to embarrass him because he thought he was alone. We have never exchanged the phrase 'I love you,' but we know it's there; actions speak louder than words.

When I was about eight years old, I played for my first top-level travel hockey team, and I noticed that after kids got up from being hurt on the ice they received applause. Well, this just delighted me, so it seemed like for a good stretch during that season at least once a game something as innocent as getting touched by a fly would flop me down to the ice like I had just been shot. After my Dad noticed that I was doing this because I adored the applause from the fans after returning to my feet, he informed me that it was not in my best interest to keep it up. He explained that, the more I acted hurt, the less tough I would be; he then compared it to the University of Vermont hockey players, whom I lived and breathed for, and asked me if I wanted to be like those guys. I emphatically answered, 'Of course!' and he explained to me that in order to be a tough guy, you have to take hits and get hurt sometimes but not show it. Dad said the UVM players never go down because they are tough hockey players. So I never went down on purpose again.

These instances influenced my belief that men are supposed to be tough, and men do not cry from pain because we can handle it. One of my prouder moments in this context happened when I broke my arm in seventh grade; I was so proud of myself for not crying. In fact, when my mom came into the locker room while my dad was getting me out of my equipment, it was obvious she had been crying, and like the strong little guy that I was I told her that I was fine and that she didn't need to cry. I felt strong, like my dad, and to this day when people ask whether or not I cried, I still take a little pride in saying that I never shed a tear.

I have a vivid memory from when I was no older than seven, and we still lived in my old house in Burlington. It was a rainy morning, and I had just woken up; I wandered toward my parents' room. As I walked in, I noticed my mother sobbing into my father's shoulder while Dad had his arm wrapped around her. I stayed at their door for twenty seconds wondering if they would notice I was there and then inched back to my room where I laid down until I heard my parents walk past my room and downstairs to the kitchen. I later found out that my cousin-in-law, who was my parents' age and married to my second cousin, had died that night at the hand of a drunk driver. I was very young and was essentially oblivious. But looking back on that memory helps me comprehend the importance of support and love showed by my father.

Dad was Mom's rock that day; he held her while she had one of the worst mornings of her life, and while I know he was upset, I also think he was focusing on how to help my mom through the difficulty of the news. So while he mourned, he simultaneously made himself a source of strength for Mom. When I went into writing this paper, I started by asking myself how my dad showed me the ways of the manly man, and how the way he acted made me associate manhood with 'manly' things. But as this paper evolved, I have realized that my dad has showed me that being a man is all about being a good role model for your kids and the people that look up to you.

My dad never intended for me to think that manhood deals with building stuff with your bare hands or being able to take a punch; my dad has showed me that manhood is about responsibility, support, accountability, love, and being someone to look up to. Yes, I learned some things along the lines of toughness and hard work, but the most important lesson my dad has taught me about being a man is selflessness and love. My dad is a man because he loves his family more than anything else in the world; my dad is a great man because he would give up almost anything to better the lives of his children; my dad has made it easy for me to grow into a good man because of the example he set that I just simply had to follow. My dad has shaped my view of what a man is by living every day with a positive attitude, a work ethic second to none and an abundance of love."

Mike learned early on about men and tears. He also reveals how something as simple as his father's praise would have made all of the difference to him as a young high school athlete.

▶ **Mike**

" 'Toughen up. Boys don't cry.'

I can picture a few events in my life where my father has definitely influenced my view of what it means to be a man, but I can also think of some times where what he has said or done is the exact opposite of what and how I think a man should act.

I believe my father started to construct my view of what it means to be a man early on. When I was quite young, I was pushed into playing sports like hockey, soccer, and baseball. I was always very busy playing sports. My father made it seem like sports were really important, whether it was playing them or watching them on TV or in person. To my father, part of being a man was appreciating sports, and in turn, I associated sports with being a guys' thing and not for girls.

I can also remember numerous times (usually playing sports) where I got hurt, or when I fell off a bike, and my father said, 'Toughen up. Boys don't cry.' If I got hurt I wasn't supposed to show emotion, I was just supposed to pretend I was okay and keep going along with what I was doing. If it was really bad, I was supposed to get the problem fixed and then go back to what I was doing. Education was very important to both my parents, but I remember the grades I got being more important to my mother than my father. To my father, sports came first and school came second.

Throughout my whole life I can only remember a handful of times when my father has shown any kind of emotion other than being angry. I don't ever remember seeing my father cry or anything like that. In some ways, I have since associated crying with being unmanly—along the same lines as the stereotype that boys don't cry. In stark contrast to my dad, I would consider myself a fairly emotional and passionate man, depending on the situation. I can never really recall my father ever being overly passionate about anything besides sports. While I am passionate about sports, I am also very interested in politics and other things that I think are important to being a man.

There is one event from my childhood that has defined everything I do and why I am so concerned with overachieving and being the best. To me, being the best is part of being a man. In high school, I started cross-country skiing. I became very good at it, to the point where I was able to represent New England at the Junior Olympics. To put making the New England Junior Olympic team in some sort of context, there are roughly 2500 children under the age of eighteen racing competitively in New England. The top fifteen athletes represent New England at the JOs. I raced the 10K mass start in the freestyle technique. A good race for me would have been a top-30 result. I would have been very happy for a top-30. As the race went on, I found myself with a skier I should not have been able to stay with. I had extremely good skis and was pretty much skiing the race of my life. With about a kilometer to go, a skier from Colorado made a move and somehow I was able to go with him. Up the final hill he just laid down the hammer, and I could not respond. He outsprinted me to the line and beat me by a boot length. I was disappointed but at the same time so happy. I had just finished in *second* place at the Junior Olympics!

I should have been nowhere near there, result-wise, but on that day I had the skis and legs to ski great. I remember being totally spent after the race, and my father came down to me at the finish. Instead of saying that he was proud of me, the first thing out of his mouth was, 'If you went a little faster on that last uphill you would have been the National Champion.' To this day, this quote from my father has made me equate being a man with winning and being the best. It means being the very best at everything you do. The idea that if you're not first you're last comes to my mind when I think about what it means to be a man. I think in some ways the reason I am so highly motivated to be the best and be the most important is because I equate that with being a man and being masculine."

***

Once again, I would suggest that many fathers are not aware of the impact that their words and actions have on their young sons. Owen has a different perspective—and also gained great insight into who his father and his mother really are.

▶ **Owen**

"Several years ago, a fast food restaurant ran a commercial featuring a song that changed the lyrics of Helen Reddy's 1970s hit 'I Am Woman' to 'I Am Man.' Reddy's song speaks of strength, wisdom, and achieving goals. This commercial remake speaks of quiche and tofu being 'chick food' and hunger for meat being a manly thing. The slogan at the end of the commercial sums up the theme of the advertisement: *The Texas Double Whopper: Eat like a man!* There has long been a connection between manhood and meat products. Men do not cook, but it is perfectly fine for a man to stand behind a flaming grill with tongs in one hand and a beer in the other. (Well, as long as there is a juicy steak sitting there and not something as vile as a veggie burger.) Luckily, because of my father, I do not take my understanding of what a man should be from television or any other form of mass media. He does not eat meat.

My father is the oldest of five children, four of them being male. His father, my grandfather, could be considered a manly man. He worked as a carpenter and taught high school shop classes. I have heard stories about him purchasing cars for two hundred dollars, putting a few hours of elbow grease (and probably some other kind of grease) into them, and selling them for three hundred. Last spring break, I spent the week not in Cancun, but in my grandfather's basement crafting wagon wheels out of wood. My father and grandfather do not share the same affinity, or skill set, for what can only be described as 'tinkering.' What they do share, though, is an incredible love and willingness to sacrifice for their families.

Growing up, my father encouraged me to play sports but did not force me. For example, I played one year of youth soccer and absolutely hated it. I always wanted to touch the ball with my hands, and my coach was mean and smoked cigarettes at practice. I hated soccer and my father was fine with that. Basketball and baseball were my favorite sports, and he was supportive in those endeavors. He enjoyed coaching my baseball teams up until Little League, when—for everyone except the players—fun seemed to take a back seat to competition and winning. I can still remember how seriously some of the parents took those games and rejoice that my father was not one of them. Sure, he wanted us to do well, but he knew it was more about having fun than anything else. My parents made it a priority to attend my sporting events as often as they could, something I am grateful for. Small things like that can really make a difference in a kid's life.

On the academic front, my father really let me do my own thing. Homework was never strictly enforced, but I do not think this meant that he did not care. It was more of a way for me to gain some responsibility and independence at a young age. Also, my father is not much of a scholar. To my knowledge, he has read two books in his life: *A Walk in the Woods,* about hiking the Appalachian Trail, and a book about prostate cancer, which he read after being diagnosed in 2007. In my experience, when people get sick, they want to do one of two things. They either want to be cured without knowing anything about what is wrong with them, or they want to learn all about their sickness and the best options for recovery. I am very glad that my father read the second book.

One thing I admire about my father is his ability to emote. Our society might say that it is not acceptable for men to cry, but any person who has lived for as long as my father should be allowed. But I have only seen my father cry once—when my sister got married. I have been told by my mother that he cried for a week straight when I moved away to college, but she may have embellished just a bit. As far as anger goes, my father keeps it to a minimum or expresses it elsewhere. The only time my father raises his voice in our house is when one of the animals has done something foolish, which happens on occasion. More notable than his ability to cry or limit his anger is his ability to love, and to show that love. My parents do this thing that really used to bother me. It's called kissing, and it happens when they get home from work. It's usually prefaced by a long embrace. I used to say things like 'gross' or 'stop that,' but I am starting to think of how nice this daily occurrence is—that just maybe the best part of my father's day is coming home and seeing the woman he has been married to for twenty-six years. If I can emulate my father in only one way I want to be able to love someone as much as he loves my mother.

I really do not know what being a man is all about. If it is truly about eating excessive quantities of meat and holding your emotions inside, then my father has failed terribly. What my father has shown me is that it is okay to go along with what you believe and what you feel. He cannot calibrate the timing belt on his Toyota, he probably cannot eat a steak without regurgitating it, and he no longer has a prostate, but my father is a great man."

Chapter 3

Fathers Who Disappoint or Distant Fathers

In my experience, most fathers do the best job they know how to do; however, that doesn't mean that they necessarily give their kids what they really need. I once led a workshop at a substance abuse treatment program in Carbondale, Colorado, and asked the thirty men there (ages 18–45) if they wanted to become fathers, someday. Each man in the room answered a resounding, "Yes"! When I then asked them why, they sat for a minute or two in stunned silence and later revealed that they hadn't given that question much thought. Each man knew that he wanted to be a dad, but did not know why. Our society strongly pressures men to be fathers without sufficient infrastructure in place to help them understand the incredible level of responsibility that fatherhood requires. One of the most recurring themes I come across in student essays is that of fathers who either disappoint their kids in a big way or fathers who are seen by their kids as being "distant." Sometimes, with patience and communication, issues arising from the disappointment or distance can be worked out. In other scenarios, the damage is too severe and the relationship cannot be repaired. When a father and a child recognize these difficulties early enough, the chances for positive change increase exponentially.

Why are some fathers emotionally distant? Why are some fathers physically distant? Again, the societal construct that places enormous value on men as primary breadwinners with successful careers also encourages men to prioritize time spent earning money as their most valuable contribution to family life—clearly, as many students reveal, this often parlays to a emotional and generational void and the detriment of family life. Emotional distance is as damaging as physical distance, and yet society has shortchanged its acceptance of men as emotionally available, connected, and active caregivers. In either case, the children of distant fathers can personalize and misinterpret this behavior as their own innate inadequacy or their fathers' lack of love or interest. In fact, when students are asked to reflect on their relationships with their fathers, praise and longing commonly fall into similar categories: "I wish my father had been there to see me play"; or conversely, "My father never missed a game."

***

Evie offers us a clear view of the "distant" father. The revisions she makes to her interpretation of her father's actions seem to point to the fact that as she grew, she became more aware of the societal pressures on her dad. After reading her paper, I asked her if she felt that her dad had any choice in his decisions—or if his construct of a man and of a father "required" him to work hard so that his family was financially sound. It's hard not to wonder what Evie and her dad missed out on as they traveled this complicated road of misunderstanding.

▶ Evie

"When I was growing up, my father spent lots of time traveling on business trips. When I was seven, my parents got divorced. After that, I only saw him every other weekend, if that. As a child and growing into my adolescence, I never understood why he always chose to travel instead of spend the weekend with my five siblings and me. In a very traditional way, my father viewed his financial contributions to our family as more important than just spending time with us. Now that I can understand his logic, comprehension of his actions is much easier. As I aged into adolescence, we grew apart; he was traveling more and I was a snotty teenager. I could not understand why he couldn't make it to my eighth grade graduation, my confirmation, or a single one of my cross-country meets. I thought he didn't care about me, but I see now that—from his point of view—he was doing the most important of his fatherly duties: working hard to support me."

***

Sometimes fathers provide their sons or daughters with models of what a man should not be. They don't do this intentionally, but kids are more observant than most parents realize and they pick things up by merely watching what is happening around them. It doesn't take much to internalize bad examples. Ashley shows us how her father's behaviors taught her what it means to be a man in today's world. And like too many young people today, her father's attitudes, values, and beliefs inform her decisions about current or potential boyfriends. Ashley seems to have been able to sort out which lessons she will keep and which ones she will reject, but what price did she pay as she learned these lessons?

▶ Ashley

"My dad always loved to explain life lessons through metaphors. Some of his best lines are, 'Every breath is a gift; every day is a celebration,' 'Never force anything,' and 'If you're not part of the solution, you're part of the problem.' But his favorite one by far is, 'A real man is he who never loses the heart of a child.' While I love this quote, over the years I have realized how my dad takes it a little too seriously. In many different ways, my father is a great man, but at the same time he is still very much a boy.

My family and I always joke that my dad stopped maturing at age thirteen, but lately it has become less of a joke and more of a complaint. My father comes off as a very happy man and always reminds my siblings and me to appreciate everything we have in life. His entire adult life he has been a bartender and a house painter. He is self-employed so he can work on his own time. He likes to be able to go golfing whenever he wants and go traveling with his friend's band if they need him, without a work schedule holding him back. He used to have a steady job working for a painting company where he would have continuous work, but that did not last long because he would always paint the houses whatever color he thought was best, not what his boss wanted. My father could never sit well with the fact that sometimes we have to do what other people tell us to. Now most of his painting jobs come from family friends at random.

Looking back at these aspects of my father, I guess he has partly shown me what I think a man should not be. Out of his three kids, I have had the hardest time getting along with him. His struggles have become our struggles because of his inability to support us financially and emotionally throughout the years. We used to have a custody plan after my parents' divorce where we would spend a certain amount of days with him each week, but that didn't last long. Now, he mainly comes by to say hello once in a while or take us out to dinner. While I am fine with this, I have thought about how I would like the father of my children to be more supportive and a more consistent worker. In the past months, I have even found myself pushing my boyfriend to sort of have a plan for after college. I have a fear of being with someone who refuses to grow up in the ways that my father did, especially now that it seems like more and more men fit the 'man-child' description of not being able to let go of their college lifestyle.

In many ways my father is exactly what most men should be, though.

When he works he works very hard and finds ways to look positively at whatever is thrown his way. My mom and dad had a terrible divorce but throughout my childhood he never let his negative feelings toward my mother get in the way of our time together. He would make something as simple as a car ride to the store exciting and even persuaded us that vegetables are enjoyable to eat. What I admire most about my father is his love for music. Every time I see him he is singing, playing the guitar, or making CDs of songs that he thinks we would love. He knows he cannot offer us a lot of material things, so he gives us gifts in the form of music. I used to wonder how a man who has had a difficult life like his can constantly stay so happy, and now I know that music helps him take a step back and appreciate what he has. He takes life with a grain of salt and has helped us to do the same, partly by showing us the beauty in music and how it can help any situation become better. This is where his 'heart of a child' is exactly what I think all men should have. It is important to see that not everything that goes wrong is the end of the world, and to not let negative experiences define your life.

My father always told me, 'Be a leader, not a follower,' and thanks to him, I know what it means to lead. He has not accomplished much financially, but he knows how to make the best of any situation. I suppose this is why I expect men to be strong, logical leaders. My father has always been able to think on his feet and has such an outgoing personality that people want to be around him and hear what he has to say.

In many ways, my father has the best and worst qualities of a child. He is stubborn, egocentric, and does not think about future consequences, while at the same time he is extremely giving of what he does have, is lighthearted, and remains very positive. He is always ready and willing to try new things and does his best to take meaning from any situation. Although I have had a hard time getting along with my father, I would definitely say his best qualities outweigh his worst qualities. He is a man and men make mistakes, and I have learned much about what a man is by remembering my father's mistakes and his lessons. My father has taught me through his faults and triumphs that a man should be a leader, be open-minded, persevere though hard times, and be able to take whatever life throws his way. Looking at whom my father is as a man, I have come to realize how much it has affected what I look for in a man. My expectations are high but it will be worth the wait if I find someone who has my father's best attributes."

***

As I was sorting out the essays, I knew that I had to include Charles's story, especially because he followed up with me a few years later. Several students have done this—written their initial essay early in our semester together and then, when they are more comfortable with me and perhaps more comfortable with themselves, they ask if they can rewrite the initial essay. Charles, a biology major and very serious student-athlete, has always been curious; he asks questions and he wants answers. We developed a friendship over several courses, and I was impressed with the level of his work in class and with his level of critical thought outside class.

▶ Charles

"Fortunately, most young boys have a father figure in their lives who helps mold their idea of what it means to be a man, however good or bad this might actually be. During my childhood, I was lucky enough to have a steady biological father in my life. From my birth, my father began to construct my idea of what a man was and what it meant to be one.

Some different elements that combine to make a man that I learned from my father are: caring, compassionate, uncompromising, intellectual, stubborn, hardworking, and tough. My father has also instilled some other ideas in me as well, mainly that it is good to respect any and all individuals. Individuals are not a means to an end, but an end in themselves. Also, the man is the breadwinner of the family.

The first lesson that I can recall being taught to me by my father was that of respect. This has greatly shaped me into the man that I am (or would like to think that I am) today, because I truly do not take individuals for granted and respect their differences. This lesson has not come easily to me and I am certainly still learning and will continue to do so for the rest of my life. Perhaps the most engrained trait of what it means to be a man that I learned from my father was to be stubborn and hardworking. I have always been stubborn and probably will be to some degree for the rest of my life.

There are also many times during my childhood that my father exemplified traits that I view now to be what a man ought not to be. For this I'm thankful because without being able to see the faults in my own father, I would not be able to see the faults in myself. Also, he has provided me with the necessary steps to modify my faults the best I can. This has allowed me to continue to change my idea of what a man is on a regular basis.

My current idea for what a man is can best be described as a compilation of traits that work together to form who I currently am today. A man is hardworking and intelligent. He is strong mentally and physically, faithful and respectful of everyone and everything. Along with being compassionate, motivated, a diligent partner in relationships, and a protector for those who cannot adequately defend themselves, I ultimately believe a man to be open and willing to change."

***

So, that essay presented an interesting and not unusual picture of what a man is or should be, and was learned from a father who is respected and admired. Charles and I have kept in touch as he has now graduated and is in graduate school. Charles's reaction to his initial writing about his father fits into a pattern that is often seen in young people. Many people, even while holding strong emotions about their fathers, hesitate to talk about, to write about, or to think about the negatives because of a fear of being "disloyal" to their parent. I am not surprised that Charles was able to rethink his views on how his father influenced his view of what it means to be a man after some time to think and experience more with his father.

▶ Charles – Part Two

"I wanted to give you an update on my perspective of what my father taught me when I was growing up. From the last time that I had written you that paper, I have had plenty of time to reflect back on my experiences and added some new ones as well.

Since my graduation from Saint Mike's, my father has continued to teach me to keep looking for new and challenging experiences, especially with athletics. Soon after returning home from college, I ended up going down to Texas to try out for a semiprofessional hockey team. Against all odds, I made it to the short list to begin playing in the exhibition games. Eventually, I was on the team and could finally call myself a professional athlete. This was the culmination of what I had been working for my entire athletic career. It was also the first time that my father gave me what would be considered by many the ultimate compliment for a hockey player—that I had finally become a complete hockey player.

Thinking back, my father has always encouraged me to grow athletically and academically, yet not in my personal life. He never had 'the talk' with me and everything that I had learned was from books, my friends, or other trusted adults. Still to this day, he does not place much value in my relationship with my current girlfriend of over six years. She is not a random 'flash in the pan'; she is the girl that I plan to marry and have a family with. What's more, my dad encourages me to make decisions with little to no consideration for her or her family. This is what really torques me because I know that kind of thinking is what allowed him to one day pack up and leave my siblings and my mother. The more I think back about it, the more it pisses me off because with him being an engineer, I know that everything he does is 'calculated' and well thought out. It is something that I have learned from my father: how not to be. But I have taken a page out of my mother's book of values: love unconditionally and wholeheartedly, no matter the consequences. I'm not sure if it is going to work out, but I am going to give it a shot and see what happens."

***

Not all fathers are biological in nature, nor are all "fathers" male. Here is Jeff's essay about his mother's influence and how she compensated for his father's absence. Albeit implicitly, Jeff's story raises a set of important questions—namely, what happens when fathers leave and then come back? When fathers attempt to reintegrate themselves into a child's life, how is the son or daughter supposed to respond? With gratitude? With perpetual fear of future abandonment? Does the mother who "stepped in to fill the void" suddenly step aside?

▶ **Jeff**
"Where I grew up, it is typical for fathers to be absent. And my father taught me just as much in his absence as he could have with his presence. Although I knew my father growing up and saw him once in a while, he wasn't always there mentally to teach me things. His father died when he was young and wasn't there the way he should have been while he was alive, and the same behaviors trickled down the family ladder.

For me, the definition of a man is: a puzzle piece. A man is a puzzle piece because it is the person who fits the open slot in this jigsaw puzzle we call life. (And I use the word 'it' with specific purpose.) Now take the time to imagine putting together a jigsaw puzzle. Notice that you can try to jam in a piece to fill the void. But if the piece doesn't fit, you can't complete the puzzle. The traditional family cycle becomes more rare every year as the divorce rate continues to climb and as more and more couples have children out of wedlock. There are also same sex marriages and relationships where females take on the male role.

My father moved out when I was six years old, and my mom had to handle the duties of both mother and father. My family was evicted from our apartment after my father didn't pay rent for the fourth time. And the cycle continued when we moved in with my Grammy. My mom had enough of the financial pitfalls and asked my father to leave. So at the age of six, I became the patriarch of the family, because I didn't have a male figure ahead of me. I had to find my way by creating my own path toward becoming a successful man because I didn't have a male figure to look up to.

Although becoming a man is something that I could only teach myself without a father figure for so many years, I still considered my mom to be the closest thing I had to a father. She was the disciplinarian, the handyperson, the provider, and the anchor of our household. She was the closest person I could look to for advice. She even taught me how to be a gentleman. But because I became the patriarch at such an early age, there wasn't much room for error. So for every mistake I made, I had to bounce back from it twice as fast. There wasn't any time to enjoy my childhood either. I had to hustle and hit the books hard. For every bit of knowledge I could garner—whether book smarts or street smarts—I couldn't miss the opportunity to obtain it. And for every door that opened up, I had to be an opportunist, trying to open more doors.

It's difficult to picture any woman being a man, physically. But figuratively? That's easy for me. My mom has so many qualities that are considered the valuable qualities of a man. She is a hardworking individual. She knows how to do handy work such as carpentry, painting, and laying down tile flooring. And while I was growing up, there was no physical male figure to look up to. This is why I think you have to look beyond the literal definition of a man to truly define it. I don't have to search much further than my mom. She has taught me how to be independent and not have to rely on a woman to do the things that women are usually forced to do based on societal values, such as cooking and cleaning. She is the person who stepped up and filled the void of the male figure in my life. And, figuratively, I think a 'man' is any person who is able to step in as that missing puzzle piece.

My father and I have a better relationship now, but that still doesn't take away from the fact that I had to learn so many of life's lessons on my own while growing up. I wish I had some of those years back with all the knowledge I have now. But unfortunately, time is the one thing we cannot gain back. Typically, we think of men as these powerful, dominant beings. But ultimately, any person can fill the shoes of a man. Women can be just as strong, supportive, and providing as a male figure. The childbearing process takes strength. The nurturing of a child exhibits a woman's supportive nature. And the way a woman goes the extra mile to provide for her child is what it takes to raise one. Both men and women are capable of the same efforts and have traces of the same qualities. It is the person— whether male or female—who is most courageous to step up to the plate and deliver."

***

Although the assignment was open-ended, most students wrote in essay format. However, Olivia organized her thoughts around five personality traits— all but one negative. Her "acceptance" that so many men are like her father causes concern for her future career and her future relationships. This is a sad reality for many students, and one of the reasons why a class like Men & Masculinities is so important. It provides young people with an opportunity to explore issues they have always kept to themselves that may have grave consequences for their future happiness.

▶ Olivia

"I have often felt uncomfortable and unsure of myself around men. Much of this discomfort seems to stem from my relationship with the first man in my life, my father. In this paper, I will explain how my father has shaped my constructs and concepts of masculinity. I will discuss several key aspects of my father's influential role on my social construct of masculinity. Moreover, I will explore how my father's actions and our relationship influenced my own perceptions. To do this, I will pick several adjectives that best describe my father's modeling, and then discuss them.

Angry

My father is frequently angry, and he has been my whole life. He struggles with depression and anxiety, as do I, but rather than displaying these disorders in a more typical way, he usually expressed them in anger. In fact, he expresses all of his negative feelings in the form of anger. My father taught me that anger is acceptable to display, even when it negatively impacts others. I think that this is one of the most influential things I have learned from my father about masculinity. I learned as a young child that being angry is a normal part of being a man. I also learned that being angry is powerful. This has made me resentful of men. I established an image of men as being unable to express any feelings other than anger, and I have provoked men in my life to become angry at me to reinforce this message.

This anger has also made me think poorly of my father's communication ability, a judgment that has carried over to how I conceive of all men. For example, I tend to think that women are more verbal and able to communicate, whereas I often perceive men to have more difficulty communicating or dealing with situations with high emotional stress. Along those lines, the idea that I cannot talk to a man when I have a problem has become part of my beliefs about men. I learned from my father's anger that men are difficult to talk to, and that, when anger emerges, I become helpless. As a defense mechanism, when men (and people, in general) become angry with me, I melt or run away. My father's anger has made me fearful of angry people, especially of men who are acting in this manner.

Frightening

Some of my earliest memories are of tears streaming down my reddened cheeks; my back pressed up flat against the wall; me begging, crying, and screaming. I recall looking at the figure before me, cheeks an angry red, eyes blazing, and practically emitting steam from his ears, like a cartoon character. In childhood, I remember often being scared, or at least unsure, of my father. Through my father's actions, I grew up frequently being scared of what my dad would think or do in a situation. My father's ability to change before my eyes, from calm to out of control, was highly influential in the formation of my opinion of men. One wrong remark and he would be all-out screaming at me. I would try to run away, desperate to leave the situation, but I was never able to get away; he would always follow me. I grew up learning to be quiet and stay out of the way. I learned that men are scary and unstable. I learned that being yelled at makes you wish you had never been born. This continual sense of fear and worry has been threaded throughout my life.

Consequently, I was taught at a young age to fear men. Not only did my father make me wary by his example, he also made me wary of strangers. I learned that I always have to remember that men have the capacity to induce verbal or physical pain. I think that growing up with an authoritarian father who I was unable to reason with, who I was scared and intimidated by, and who became frighteningly angry, made me extrapolate scared feelings to many men in my life. The combination of anger and fear has continued and has instilled an innate sense of wariness and distrust of men.

Dismissive

Coupled with his angry and scary tendencies, my father modeled disrespect. He belittles my ability to think independently and disagree with him. He tears me down into a pit of nothingness, and his yelling evokes feelings of being valueless. This behavior creates raw wounds. It makes me feel voiceless and boils the bubbling pot of anger inside me. By these actions, my father has taught me that men are disrespectful and that being treated badly is normative. Because of this image, I have often dated or been friends with men who did not treat me well, who disrespected me, or who made me feel worthless. The power differential between my father and me has created a model of men being on a higher plane. My father's dismissals of me have made me internalize this image of masculinity.

When I am completely honest with myself, I find that I still want a man to be in control. I want someone to pursue me, rather than the other way around. I expect to be disrespected by men, particularly by the men I love. Because my earliest interactions were often dismissive and controlled, I learned a different set of standards of what I would accept from male partners. My father's interactions with me are very similar to a line in the Cat Stevens song—'From the moment I could talk, I was ordered to listen." I, too, always had to listen, and I struggled to have my voice heard.

Along with accepting disrespect, my father taught me that I was never the most important person. He was emotionally unavailable; he would only let me talk about my day during commercial breaks. He taught me that men do not, or should not, care. He constructed an image of manhood that was often emotionally distant, apathetic, and even cold. Moreover, my father's own need to always have the last word and always be right was entirely dismissive of different points of view. Last fall I was studying for the GRE, and I asked my father to please be a little quieter when he was making dinner. This request kicked off an hour-long argument about what I had said, and how I was rude and disrespectful. When I refused to apologize, he told me repeatedly that I was wrong and he was right, because he could not be wrong in his own home. When my father is upset, arguing becomes a moot point. This image of being forced to kowtow to men has made me resentful. In other ways, my father's example that men always have the last word has silenced and crippled me.

Controlling

My father struggles to maintain control in his job, his family, and in his personal relationships. He frequently displaces his anger on the family when he feels a lack of control in some other aspect of his life. At times, the search for control is subtler, such as holding on to the television remote and refusing to let anyone else touch it. At other times, my father is more obvious about his control. My father has said repeatedly that he is the king and the home is his castle; I am simply a person staying there who does not contribute anything. My father also becomes instantaneously defensive when he feels that his power is being in any way tested or usurped. It becomes a problem when I attempt to talk back during an argument or even try to have a response other than the desired two-word affirmative of 'Okay, Dad.'

My father's control issues have made me believe that all men desire control. Additionally, I see this male control everywhere: from the guy with two girls draped on his arm, the male student who silences dialogue by calling a girl a 'bitch' or 'slut,' or the way that my ex-boyfriend wanted to control and change me to better fit the idea of the kind of girlfriend he wanted. The image of control has become utterly integrated into my image of masculinity. Additionally, my father's own controlling ways have changed the way I relate to men. Control is a very serious issue, and because I was under his control for years, it is now extremely important for me to be in control. Moreover, my father's example of this has instilled a deep sense of rebelliousness and hatred for male control.

Inconsistent

Writing this paper, all of the adjectives that came to mind were negative. In many ways, this is reflective of the relationship between my father and me, which is often strained at best. At times, however, my father has shown me positive images of masculinity or what a man is supposed to be. For example, I learned a sense of gentleness from my father when I watched him make a cake with my three-year-old second cousin. I also learned that men can be kind and caring, from the way he calls daily to ask if I need anything on his way home from school. My father has also depicted loyalty in the many times he has stood up for me when I could not. Such as when a friend hit me on the school bus, when a neighbor yelled at me, or when I have had roommate issues in college. My father has a tendency to wholeheartedly take my side when he feels I am being threatened. I think that his actions have molded my image of masculinity in this way. I value loyalty above all, and I view being loyal and protective as very admirable masculine characteristics. I think that these actions provided a paradigm that men in my life should want to protect and care for my best interest.

My father's vacillation of moods has made me unsure of men. He can be difficult to be around because one day he is fun and caring, and the next day he is bitter and sullen. Additionally, my father acts very differently when other people are around. In front of others, he is often charming and funny, but when he is at home he is much more difficult. My father's change in moods showed me that men are unstable, and that I need to walk on eggshells around them. Because my father can be very caring and loving, as well as mean and damaging, I always have the desire to work through things after a fight. My father's rapid changes in moods and behaviors have made me addicted to the good times and completely fearful of doing something to turn the tide. My father has depicted an image of masculinity that is, at times, wonderful, but always difficult to decipher."

***

Grace's father did disappoint, and he was absent, in many different ways. Her essay reveals the price she paid (and perhaps continues to pay) because of her father's influence and modeling behavior. Grace shows us the effect that divorce can have—as she so aptly puts it in her title, the results are tragic.

▶ **Grace**
The Tragic Flaws
I was six when my parents got divorced, and I developed selective

sensory deprivation shortly thereafter. I tuned out most of the fights and meanness; many things my sisters remained witness to I was happily unaware of. My father was not a 'natural' at fatherhood, and he was definitely not prepared for girls. Dad's method of single parenting treated us as something roughly between military school cadets and feral cats—we could light single-match fires and build teepees, march in time, and distinguish the edible plants in the backyard for snacks. We all tried to be better than a real son.

My first experiences of my father's expectations of masculinity were applied directly to me: Be active and capable, not a wuss or a crybaby. Calm is better than chatty, silent is best of all. We did mandatory pull-ups and push-ups, and wore military-issue jumpsuits over swimsuits for weeks on end in the summer. Our Barbies quickly received the Demi Moore crew cut and were clad in leaves and grass like Amazons. For Christmas and birthdays, we received pocketknives, .22 rifles, soap, and underwear. We were mocked for spending too much time in the bathroom 'primping.' In fact, the first present from him that was remotely feminine was a strand of pearls for my high school graduation, which still seem out-of-place on me.

To my father's deep and continuing dismay, instead of becoming a gun-toting, number-crunching Tea Party libertarian, I became a sex-positive liberal feminist (about to graduate with a degree in 'victimhood' that qualifies me 'to sue any company in the country for sexual harassment and discrimination'). Manly he is; feminist he is not.

For a long time, my view of men was that they were supposed to be kind of jerks. Arrogance and machismo attracted and enraged me; I recognized and hated those qualities in my father but seemed to seek them out in my boyfriends. Things that should have come easily for a burgeoning feminist took me a long time to figure out: that I could demand respect from a man, for one. Even now, I find myself surprised—and not a little suspicious—when a man does something unexpectedly considerate for no apparent reason.

I dated men who were arrogant, commanding, and manly; men I knew my dad would hate on sight, but who reminded me of him. I distrusted men and broke the hearts of a few who couldn't make it past the damage. In high school, I embraced the man-hater stereotype, partly because I didn't know how to respond to that sort of 'teasing' without laughing and going along, but partly because I had a lot of resenting to do, and it was so easy. Starting college, I switched tracks and tried to sleep my way through the feelings of abandonment and rejection.

Years of our not speaking made it difficult for my father to influence my view of masculinity in positive ways during a pretty formative time. What I knew of him mostly consisted of vague childhood memories, the embittered observations of my mother, and his obvious and painful absence from my life—made more agonizing by his frequent contact with my sisters.

The summer of 2008 changed all of that, kind of. My sister informed me that Dad was sad that I had ignored all the letters he'd sent me over the years. This was funny, because I never received anything but court-mandated checks from him—the first came with court papers to prove that it was nothing more than obligatory. My mother assures me to this day that she never threw anything from him away. Regardless of the existence of actual letters, the incident prompted me to write a less-than-cordial e-mail, and the first real communication between us in four or five years began.

It was ugly.

He called me disrespectful, greedy, ungrateful, and aggressively contemptuous. I said he was condescending and kidding himself if he thought he could throw money at me and expect a relationship to suddenly appear.

We never discussed the content of those e-mails again. Ever. And yet our relationship restarted, as if we just needed to get those things off our chests for our hearts to start beating again. Mind you, it's not all cuddles and I-Love-You's sprinkling the fairy-land of Normalcy, but we manage regular, albeit brief, communication and family-bonding time. It was sometime after that encounter that I pieced together the fragments and came up with this: Our relationship was stunted because he was a man, not because I wasn't. All those years of feeling inadequate and unwanted were a product of crossed signals: he didn't know how to connect with any of us, and I was too young, then too hurt, then too stubborn to understand. I won't say it's been revolutionary; the past has been so internalized, and not all of the ugliness in it was because of simple misunderstandings. But there is something there now, a truth I can come back to when the old feelings rear their heads: His shortcomings as a father, and as a man, are not malicious. They are tragic."

Stan comes to understand some harsh realities when his father's comments "free" him to make his own decisions about relationships and what it means to be masculine (instead of obediently and unquestioningly following his dad's decisions).

▶ Stan

"When I was growing up, my father, as would be expected, was my idol. I wanted to be a cop because he was a cop. I played hockey because he played hockey. We both liked the Bruins and the Yankees, but we hated the Red Sox, and more than anything, we hated the Whalers. We would go to Hartford to see Whalers' games just to root for the other team. Besides the superficial stuff, I learned a lot from my dad. One of the most important things (as I would find out later in life and eventually have to find ways to deal with) was how he treated women, specifically my mother. Watching him taught me the value of the people around me; a lesson that eventually encompassed all people, not just the women in my life. I learned the value of taking responsibility for my actions. It still surprises me how often people are unwilling to apologize. I also learned the value of both having an opinion and not having an opinion, and the force and timing in which to use either strategy.

When I was growing up, we always ate family dinner. Years later, my mom and sister would tell me how much they hated it. The food was good when my dad cooked (my mom burned everything), but the conversation was completely dominated by my dad and me. We would argue for hours about something stupid, usually right through doing the dishes. I can't remember any of the things we talked about. Most dinners ended with my mom having a couple of glasses of wine and not talking and my sister trying to enter the discussion, us disagreeing, and her running to her room and slamming the door. This was a typical night.

Hockey is something that I've been very careful not to think about at all because I don't want it to stop being meaningful. Every year, my dad and I go to Boston to see the Bruins play the day after Thanksgiving. One year we saw them beat the Islanders 7-2 in one of the most entertaining hockey games I've ever seen. As a kid, I could never get really excited about the games because I didn't see the difference between watching them on TV and going to them. I could tell how happy my dad was when I jumped out of my seat this time and started yelling after a goal. I had to choke back tears when I realized how he must have been feeling in that moment. Thinking about why hockey makes me happy will ruin it. I have to allow myself that mindless pleasure. It will always be difficult for me to recognize that I make him happy just because I'm alive.

My dad always treated my mom like gold. There was nothing more important in his life than his family. It was the number one thing that he relied on and more important, that he knew his family was relying on him. The most difficult conversation I've ever had with my father was when I told him that this most important lesson was no longer true. I knew my parents were going to get divorced before they did, but the way that my dad went about it was destructive to my view of him and my view of masculinity. Without going into the details, I found myself in a place where I needed to tell him what my view of his actions with another woman was. I explained to him how he had been my idol, and how whenever I took a girl out I had what he would do in the back of my mind. I had to tell him that I didn't think that anymore.

A few years later I was just getting out of a long-term relationship, and I met my dad for lunch in a dive bar in Greenwich Village. We talked for a while and I explained to him my frustrations with the girl I was dating. He tried to help me as much as he could, but in the end he yet again became an example of what not to do. He told me that, in college, Friday and Saturday had been for my mom. He told me that Sunday through Thursday afternoon were all about school. And he told me that Thursday night was for him.

As I began to see what he was insinuating, I recognized that he might actually be telling me it was okay to cheat on my girlfriend in order to make sure that I was both happy and fulfilling a commitment I'd made. This was the moment where my dad freed me to make decisions on what it meant to be masculine for myself.

Something that happened recently made me realize that I am satisfied with the decisions I have made for myself in this way. A friend had felt comfortable calling me at 9 am to go help her jump her friend's car. I had jumper cables, and I knew how to do it. Neither of them knew how to get to the battery, or how to hook up the cables, or what might be wrong, or where to go to get a new battery. I knew all of that. I had the knowledge that I needed to help my friend, and more important, I had become someone who my friends could depend on. As I walked back to my townhouse with all of this running through my head, I found myself thinking, 'Hey, I think I could be a dad.' It was a thought that made me happy, and I didn't know why. I felt completely comfortable with my own views on masculinity and that I fulfilled them well. Like I said, I may not always like the example that my dad gave me about what it is to be a man in the culture I've grown up in, but I know I'm happy with the pieces that I've taken away from him."

***

It is never easy to sort out which of the messages we receive about what a man should be like are real and which ones are the product of wishful thinking. Ben's wish that his father had taught him how to shave was so poignant to me that it became the title for this book. When, for whatever reason, fathers decide to leave a family, that sense of abandonment rears its ugly head. Because of a typical lack of communication over these issues, children often spend an inordinate amount of time knowing something is wrong but not knowing exactly what it is. Like Ben, they often question in silence or run into "family secrets" that prevent them from being given an honest answer.

▶ Ben

"I am unsure of what a man is. Using adjectives to determine what a man is or is not can be challenging. I have difficulty answering the question. I once viewed a man as someone who is respectful, hardworking, intelligent, strong, and self-sufficient. However, these characteristics could be identical to a description of what a woman is. If a woman embodies these qualities, is she a man? The labels that we apply to gender tend to corner us into old methodologies that we should try to escape. However, evading these socially constructed views is easier said than done. In the future, I wonder if questions defining the differences between men and women are no longer going to be asked.

My dad is the stereotypical traveling businessman: business suit, leather briefcase, Rolex, and his finger armed and ready to push the trigger of his World Edition Blackberry. He has been this way ever since I was young. For several weeks at a time, he would venture off to foreign destinations conducting important business with customers abroad. I never questioned why he took weeklong hiatuses from the house, or contemplated what he was doing in China, the Congo, or Chile. In my eyes, my father's job was his identity. His busy traveling schedule became as second nature to me as staying in fancy hotels and flying first class is to him.

My relationship with my father is strongly correlated with the amount of time he spent traveling. As a result, I feel like I have never experienced some aspects of a father-son relationship. Although it seems trivial, I wish my father taught me how to shave. As a child, I remember watching movies depicting a father and son lathered with white foam at adjacent sinks, shaving for the first time. This was an experience that I wanted to have with my father. It meant more than just a chance to spend some time with him. This experience would have been an opportunity for my father to help facilitate my conversion from boyhood to manhood.

Not having my dad around was a struggle for my mother. I can remember overhearing one particular instance when my mom was crying to my dad saying she 'couldn't do this anymore.' As a child that meant little to me, other than I did not like to hear my mom cry. In retrospect, I understand that my mom was completely burnt out—exhausted from taking care of three boys. She raised three hungry, growing, emotional monsters practically on her own.

Around middle school, I began bragging about my dad to my friends. In fact, I grabbed one of his business cards from his desk at home. I carried that card in my blue and red Spider Man wallet like it was my own. When my friends' parents would ask me what my father did, I would reach for the business card and recite his title. I was proud of that title even though I had no concept of what it meant. The rationale for my pride was that if my dad was traveling so much, he must be important.

Contrastingly, I did not brag to my friends about what my mom did when I really should have. She took my brothers and me to practice, helped us with homework, made dinner, and made sure that we made it to the bus on time for school. In fact, my mom should have won a Nobel Peace Prize for some of the fights that she stopped between us. This realization pains me to think about because I did not appreciate what my mother has done for my family. As a child, I completely undervalued the responsibilities that she had. The sacrifice that my mother made is something I have never spoken to my parents about, but I plan to in the future.

I believe that my father inadvertently assumed the role of the provider in my family. Much of this could be a by-product of what he perceived growing up. Due to the gender-specific roles on the farm where he grew up, my father was imprinted with a socially constructed tradition where men provide and women take care of the house. This is something that he learned from his father and has trickled down from father to son for many generations.

I do not aim to portray my father as a sexist male who sentenced his wife to an eternity of providing care for men. In contrast to that image, my father treats my mother with complete respect and worships the ground that she walks on. Essentially, my father and mother fell into a social construct that was not their own.

A main contributor that helped foster my father's role in my family was his job. In the beginning of my parents' marriage, my mother and father both were employed. My father worked for a steel company and my mother was a nurse. My father was rapidly advancing in the company and was earning more money than my mother. With three boys to be raised, one of my parents was forced to make a sacrifice. In this, my mother gave up her career as a nurse while my father continued his steady path up the business ladder. Financially, it made sense for my father to work. In their case, it made more sense for a man to monetarily provide for a family and for a woman to stay at home and take care of three boys.

Reflecting on the roles that my father and mother have played in my life has opened my eyes. Although my father fell into a preordained gender role, he has still taught me what it means to be a good person. Through my father's actions, he has conveyed characteristics that make him a remarkable individual. Some of these qualities include: hardworking, intelligent, caring, emotional, committed, driven, and confident. These are traits that I have always admired my father for having. I am constantly in pursuit of mimicking each facet of my father's character, integrating them into an identity of my own. Although I sometimes waver from this goal, I feel that I embody some of these features as well. However, these are not qualities that I associate with being a man. Instead, they are values and a set of morals that encompass, in my eyes, what it means to be a good person. Being a good person is something I cherish more than anything else in my life. In conclusion, I may not know what it means to be a man. However, I believe that I have a conclusive concept of what it means to be a good person."

You can see from Ben's essay that he respects and admires his father. He wants to be like his father, and he strives to mimic his father's characteristics. At the same time, Ben never fully realized the role that his mother played in the family. With Dad away on business so much, Mom compensated for Dad's absence. Not long after Ben graduated, he shared that his mother recently discovered that her husband, who Ben believed "worshipped the ground she walks on," had been visiting porn sites and strip clubs for many years. Additionally, although he initially denied it, he had also been with a number of prostitutes over the years of his extensive travels. When Ben's mother shared this with him, it was completely devastating. Ben now questions everything about his father and everything that he has admired and respected. He questions his own relationship with his long-term girlfriend and worries that he is destined to repeat his father's actions. As you can see, when dads disappoint the effects can be far-reaching. I have to wonder if fathers truly understand the powerful implications and consequences of their actions.

Chapter 4

Fathers and Alcohol

I was raised in a home where alcohol was seemingly as important as most other things. My father was Catholic and my mother was Presbyterian, and they had agreed early on in their marriage that the boys would go to church with my father and the girls would go with my mother. As things worked out, we (the boys) went to religious instruction once a week, made our First Communions and Confirmations, and attended mass every Sunday. Dad would drive us boys to Saint Mary's Catholic Church in Auburn, New York, and we would join up with my grandmother, my aunt, and my uncle. (My grandfather had died when I was quite young, and from all reports, they held a real Irish Catholic wake for him—they talked about moving the casket out onto the porch so there would be enough room for the booze inside.)

After church, we would all go to my grandmother's home and get situated in the living room with Coca-Colas and snacks. After some brief socializing, my uncle, who didn't drink, would leave and head home to his wife and kids. As soon as my uncle was out the door, my grandmother, aunt, and father would head to the kitchen. There, they each consumed at least one shot of whiskey and a bottle of beer. This was right after the morning mass had ended.

At the time, we never questioned this weekly ritual—shots and a beer after mass. But my dad, my grandmother, my aunt, my mother's brother, and most likely my grandfather were all, if I were to put a label on them, drunks. That's the term we used to call people who were, in reality, alcoholics. Living with an alcoholic is a powerful thing; it means there are even more family secrets than in other families.

Our family secrets came to light some twenty-two years after my father died. My dad stopped his drinking by dying at the age of fifty-two, leaving a wife, three sons, and a daughter. I was fifteen. More than two decades later, while attending the wedding of one of my nephews, Dad and his drinking came up in a conversation between my siblings and me. What we discovered was that while my dad was in the hospital recovering from his heart attack, our doctor had told my mom that since "Paul has had a shot of whiskey most days of his life," it would be fine for us to take him a shot of whiskey while he was in the hospital. My mother, being a very good enabler, thought it was an even better idea to take him two shots every day. We would dutifully head to the hospital after Mom got out of work, and we would take Dad two shots of whiskey. What we discovered at my nephew's wedding is that one of my brothers was also taking Dad two shots of whiskey every day, and so were his buddies from the Post Office, and his sister. So while recovering from a heart attack in the hospital, he was consuming eight shots of whiskey every day. It is little wonder that he died two days after returning home.

A couple of years after his death, one of my aunts asked me why my mother had stayed with my father all those years, given his drinking. I was stunned at her question, as no one had ever spoken about my dad's problem. Not my mom, not my older brothers, not anyone. The family secret was well protected. If you are raised in an alcoholic home, you learn a lot about how to survive, and one of the messages you learn early on— either because you are told directly or because you learn the hard way—is that you don't talk about the drinking.

Over the many years when I was a counselor, I cannot count the number of young people who were confused, angry, saddened, curious, fearful, and in some cases, consumed with trying to find out more information about fathers and alcohol. Writer and speaker Claudia Black has written and researched extensively on adult children of alcoholics, and her work has certainly had a strong influence, not only on my own life and my comprehension of my father, but also on my understanding of how alcoholism has affected my students. I will always be very grateful to Black for her insight and friendship. Her groundbreaking book, *It Will Never Happen to Me*, published in 1996, powerfully describes the coping skills and survival techniques that are used by children of a parent struggling with addiction. Black explains that, although many of these children have travelled through adolescence and appear to have survived the problems and hardships of growing up with addicted family members, in some significant ways, theirs is an incomplete success. They have inherited a legacy of survival rules: "Don't talk; don't trust; don't feel." Despite the fact that these three messages likely served them well as vulnerable children in a challenging home environment, these "survival rules" later prove to be stunting and maladaptive when brought into healthy adult relationships. We expect our colleagues, our friends, our partners, our students, to trust us, to talk to us truthfully, to share and express feelings sincerely. Adult children from alcoholic or addicted families are often full of self-doubt and struggle with relationships that don't last because they abide by "rules" that impede their ability to communicate openly and honestly—and trust that they will be heard and cared for by the people they work with, know, or love.

The current data indicate that one in four college students comes from a home where one or both parents are alcoholics. This disturbing statistic makes me fear how many young people are blaming themselves for parental behaviors that are the result of drinking. This mistaken interpretation leads to a terrible cycle of guilt and shame that is difficult to break. The following essays will reveal how alcohol has a part to play in many of my students' views of a man.

***

Jen's essay shows us, once again, the generational nature of fatherhood behaviors—this time relating to alcohol use. According to Black, each individual member of an alcoholic's family interprets the alcoholic's behavior differently. Black's seminal works on adult children of alcoholics, especially It Will Never Happen to Me, spell out the different types of behaviors that children exhibit— whether it is through lying, as Jen did to her sister; making threats, as their mother did; pushing all of that anger inside; or taking anger out on others or one's self through self-destructive behaviors.

▶ Jen

"My father is a great man, and there is no other man in the world who could replace him. But my relationship with him has been an emotional roller coaster with many ups and downs. Sometimes I wish I could go back in time to my childhood when I used to look at my father as a hero with flawless qualities. Of course, sometimes the toughest part about growing up is reality, and reality certainly taught me that my hero was actually 'flaw-full,' if you will. Throughout my life, my father has battled a terrible addiction that I once thought would take his life. I have witnessed my sick father, and I have, fortunately, witnessed my sober father—but these two fathers have managed to show me that a man is only human.

My dad is the second oldest of six children. My grandfather was a very successful businessman who provided the family with a very comfortable lifestyle. My dad grew up in a house where his dad was the breadwinner who was rarely home. My grandfather was the boss of the house, and he did as he pleased. My dad watched his mother attend to his father's every need, and he felt sorry for her. My grandfather woke up in the morning to my grandmother's freshly squeezed orange juice and homemade breakfast. In fact, it was rare that my grandfather ate a meal that wasn't home-cooked by my grandmother. My dad's father had sports cars, traveled to Europe, and flew the family in his own plane to their Nantucket house in the summers; the children all went to private schools and had a pool and tennis courts in their backyard.

In addition to all these luxuries, my dad had an angry father with a terrible temper. My dad grew up in a house where his father physically abused his children, and my dad got it the worst. My dad was raised by anger, and he grew up to be angry himself. When I hear stories about my dad going to four different high schools, or that he was kicked off his hockey team in Switzerland, or of the hundreds of fistfights he's gotten himself into, I am really not surprised. I believe that it was the relationship that my father had with his father that influenced how my dad is today. My dad struggles to maintain civil relationships with each of his siblings because they have all been affected by their past in some way. The one relationship that has been stable for my dad throughout his life was the one he had with alcohol, and thus, he became an alcoholic.

My dad married my mother and is the father of five children. I don't know how old I was when I caught on to my dad's drinking problem, but the older I got the more I realized how bad it really was and how much it affected my family. My mom always threatened to me that she couldn't take it anymore, and it made me feel so helpless. My dad has driven drunk hundreds of times and has even wrapped one of his cars around a tree. His anger comes out more than ever when he drinks, and it carries over to his hangover the next day. I remember being a freshman in college when one of my younger sisters called me hysterically crying to tell me that my dad didn't come home the night before. He was taken by ambulance to the hospital after blacking out and getting into a fight. He tried lying to my sister's face that his cab got into an accident, but we all knew the truth. I found myself continuing the cycle of anger because I realized how angry I was at my dad.

My father took many aspects of how he was raised and brought it into his own family, but I also believe that it's the relationship that my father had with his father that made him want to be a better husband and father. When I was growing up, my parents' roles in the family looked a lot like my dad's parents' roles. My dad supported the family while my mom stayed at home, which, with five children, is debatably more than a full-time job. My mom was the one who woke up at night when we were babies, she did all the cleaning and cooking, drove us to where we needed to be, and basically kept the house functioning. It wasn't until I was twelve years old that my mother changed the dynamic in our house and began her own business, which meant that my dad was no longer the breadwinner of the house. I remember my father was so angry with this, but really, my mom had no choice. She told me a few years ago that the reason she made the decision to work was because his drinking was so bad, she knew if anything ever happened to him, we would have been in a terrible situation.

Two years ago, my dad was laid off from his job not once but twice in the same year because of his disease. My dad has attempted sobriety before but only lasted a few months. On April 21, 2010, my mom held an intervention for my father with a therapist, his siblings, his mother, and one of my brave sisters. As my dad listened to the members of his family express their concerns, he shook his head in denial while he let out some large sighs. When it was my eighteen-year-old sister's turn to speak, she spoke for the five of us. As her words came pouring out with emotion, my sister recalls he simply looked defeated. He looked her in the eye and said, 'I'm sorry for failing you guys, buddy. I never knew that it affected you and your siblings so much.' He stood up to hug her as he whispered thank you in her ear and that he was going to change.

My father has certainly not failed us. My father has been sober for almost a year now because he is devoted to making my life better. As tacky as this may sound, I don't need to go back in time to my childhood because my father is still my hero today. He has been there for us when we have needed him the most, and he has supported us in all that we do. He has adjusted his life for those who he cares about, even when his role as a man in our house was challenged. Through his weaknesses I have seen his strengths. In fact, he has shown me what a man is. A man is only human."

***

For children of an alcoholic parent, sorting out all the conflicting emotions is not an easy task. Many of these sons and daughters learn early on, as author Claudia Black observes, the rule "Don't talk, don't trust, don't feel." There is a reluctance, even a fear, of telling anyone else (even those living in the same house) that there is a problem. Ingrid, luckily, is able to see beyond her father's alcoholism, so she doesn't condemn all men because of his actions. She has come to accept that there are things she simply cannot change.

▶ Ingrid

"I'm often puzzled by the fact that I have such a negative relationship with my father yet such a positive image of men in general. I think the reason for this is the positive relationships I've had with other men in my life—my brother, my best friend from home, other men I've worked with, etc. I'm incredibly thankful for this because, if my entire vision of masculinity came from images of my father, I would have to assume that men as a whole are generally disappointing. This isn't to say I haven't absorbed any positive vibes from my dad, but most of our interactions have proven to be on the negative side.

When I was younger, I thought my dad was the best, and to be honest, when I was younger, he was. My mom worked nights; Dad would come home from work, make us our own dinner and we'd play games, go to playgrounds and swing, and read. Even when my brother was born, Dad continued to be great. He was always around, always wanted to do fun, spontaneous things like plant Mom a garden full of mums on a random summer afternoon, wash the car (which was fun to me as a kid, apparently), go buy more books to read, or find the best ice- cream cone in a thirty-mile radius.

I can't pinpoint exactly when it happened, but it was sometime around when Dad got more stressed with owning his own business that he returned to drinking, which had been a problem when he was younger but had stopped when I was born. He started to not come home at night because he would drink alone in his office, going over numbers. This culminated on Christmas Eve when I was ten; he came home, finally, at 11 PM and walked around the upstairs of my house drunk. When he fell down our stairs, I actually realized what was going on. He had been doing these types of things for probably two years at this point, but this was when it started to make me mad. I didn't want to be around this guy who wasn't my dad as I knew him; I didn't like that he clearly had stopped respecting my mom, and that he wasn't as fun as he used to be. If I had to define a man by my dad at that point, it would've been someone messy and irresponsible.

His behavior continued to get worse as I grew up, and I all but stopped speaking to him entirely. He knew that I didn't like what he was doing, and when it comes to my dad, I can be incredibly unforgiving. He started to say he would do things and would never follow through—a trait very unlike the dad I had been growing up with. He hit what I thought was the worst during my sophomore year of college, and I decided that Christmas that I wanted to talk to him again. We had a great conversation that Christmas Eve, when he was sober, and I continued from then on to make an effort. He lost his business that spring but still had hope and ideas for what to do next. I was thinking, maybe this is rock bottom? Maybe this is an opportunity to get out of this, actually get sober, change career paths, and turn things around. None of that happened, and I'm again back at a point where I just don't have anything to say. I feel incredibly distant from him and am frankly a little tired of making an effort for someone who can't seem to give that effort back, which brings me to my first claim about masculinity that I learned from my father: men are disappointing.

On another negative note, my father's example makes me think that men are inconsistent and unpredictable. We don't know what my dad's mood will be on any given day, or how he will react to any situation. On one hand, not having expectations of him anymore makes me less angry with him— I'm not surprised by much of what he does anymore—but on the other hand, I feel like I miss out on opportunities to build our relationship back up by not trying to hope for better.

I know that men overall are not disappointing and inconsistent, which is why I'm thankful that my impression of men comes not solely from my father. On a positive note, there are good things that I've learned from my dad. Underneath it all, I think he's one of the most sensitive people I know and he spent a lot of time in his business trying to 'help people out' by discounting their services, working out payment plans, and being sympathetic to the various constraints of his customers. However, I think I learned from this a sense of taking care of people. As much as it feels like my dad has lacked in taking care of me, I know that at one time he had the best of intentions for everyone. I believe that generally all humans are well-intentioned, but I have this specific example from my dad.

Overall, I really hate sounding like a girl that has 'daddy issues'; in reality, I don't think about it that much unless I'm confronted with it while I'm visiting home or someone brings up something specific. I don't have a problem with men or any of the other typical 'daddy issues' that people talk about. If my vision of masculinity was based solely on my interactions with my father, men would be equally disappointing, inconsistent, irresponsible, caring, flexible, and motivated. My lack of relationship with my dad doesn't have to do with his gender; I'm really more fed up with the situation than I am anything else. I do know and recognize that there are great parts of my dad, and I don't relate his frustrating parts to the fact that he is male, but just to his personality as a whole."

***

We see in Rose's essay that over time, alcohol abuse can change a person's personality and behavior. Sometimes those changes are subtle, and we don't see them right away; othertimes, they hit us over the head.

▶ Rose

"To understand how my view of a man was socially constructed, it is important to go over how I grew up and the experiences that I had. The way my father grew up also has to do with how I think of him as a man. While I was growing up, my dad played a very strong, active role in my life. As I was the youngest and only girl, I automatically was 'daddy's little girl.' I just wanted to please my dad. From a young age, I started riding horses, something my dad had been involved in growing up. It didn't take long for my dad to realize that I had caught the horse bug, so for my thirteenth birthday my parents bought me my first horse. My dad's father had a lifelong love for horses, and my dad loves the fact that I keep his father's love alive through riding and participating in the equestrian sport.

In my opinion, being a man means being involved with family, being emotionally strong, and being loving. My dad always instilled the values of responsibility, respect, and class in whatever we did together. He taught me to put my whole heart into everything that I loved, and I truly admire that about him. His father had a dream that my dad and his brother would take over his company and that it would be successful. My dad put his whole heart into opening a branch of the company in Vermont and has, indeed, become successful. For most of my life, my dad has been driven professionally. He has taught me that to be a successful man in his business it takes responsibility and class. He proved himself as a man by providing for my family, and I am so grateful for the life that I have had so far.

My dad grew up in an average family with average issues. My grandfather was an alcoholic, so that was something that from an early age my dad never wanted to be. My father is not one to fall into an addictive behavior pattern because he saw the strain that it put on his family and his father's health. That being said, my father started smoking cigarettes in high school to 'fit in.' He was a little bit overweight compared to the other kids, so he used cigarettes to help stop him from eating as much. This became a gateway into smoking cigarettes regularly. He wanted to fit in with the popular crowd.

I started to unravel the conflicting messages once I went to college. I started asking more questions like, Why would you be peer pressured to fit in? Were all of the guys around you smoking? I think my dad needed to have a sense of belonging to an 'elite' group of people. I think everyone in high school wants to be a part of a social group, whether that is a sports team, drama club, or language club. We all have the need to belong and to belong to something.

Up until my sophomore year, I had a pretty straightforward answer to the question of how my dad shaped my view of what a man is. But I went home for Christmas break that year, and something was drastically wrong with my father's behavior. He was participating in activities that he normally would not engage in. He started going out late and claimed that he was having drinks with friends. It seemed bizarre; he was never a big drinker, and he was always out with friends 'drinking.' The day before Christmas Eve 2009, my father did not come home. This was the tip of the iceberg that led to my parents divorcing. I will not go into detail about the events, but this was the hardest and most painful part of my life. My view of what a man and what a father are drastically changed.

The responsible, family-oriented person who I had known for nineteen years suddenly became someone completely foreign. Responsibility and family took a backseat to his life then and continue to do so. If my grandfather were around to see how my father was living his life, he would be appalled. The reason that I am bringing my parents' divorce to light is because I have never shared this on behalf of a class before, and my conception of how I grew up changed in an instant. I openly admit that I took for granted the role that a father plays in a family. It was just so strange waking up on Christmas morning, shell-shocked that my dad was not there waking us up to open stockings.

In the past two years my father has made it very clear that he will do exactly what he wants to do when he wants to do it. The man who I thought I knew is not the person I know now. It is still a raw topic to think about, talk about, or write about, but I think this is the best way to get out how I truly feel about my father. I am angry with him that he filled my head with this great picture of what a man should be and then didn't live up to it. I lived for nineteen years thinking he was that person.

I hope one day my dad will realize where he went wrong and acknowledge it. I think, ultimately, being a man means knowing when you are wrong and owning up to it. I hope one day he can own up to the fact that he ripped a perfectly wonderful family apart."

Chapter 5

Fathers and LGBTQ *(Lesbian, Gay, Bisexual, Transgendered, Questioning)* **Issues**

The mother of one of my gay students told me that she didn't want her son to tell his father that he was gay. She explained that her husband, a "good Irish Catholic", could never accept their son's homosexuality. She also said that her reasoning for keeping this family secret was that she loved her husband and she loved her son, and she didn't think that she could stand what she predicted would be her husband's reaction. She was a recovering alcoholic and her husband was an active alcoholic, and she knew that she wouldn't be able to continue to love her husband if his reaction to their son was accompanied by his drinking. She begged me to help her son understand why her wishes were best. As always, those decisions are not made by me, but by the students themselves. While he was initially angry, this student eventually came to believe that his mother's wisdom was correct: He was away at college and would never return to live at home anyway, and his mother had little choice in the matter. Out of respect and love for his mother, this young man didn't say anything to his father about his sexual orientation. The mother in this story died shortly after these discussions, but a couple of years later, the father did acknowledge that his son was gay.

Another one of my current students has not told her father that she is a lesbian on the advice of her mother, who warned her that if she came out to her dad, he might stop paying for her college education. The price that this student has to pay for, in her words, "being inauthentic" is very high. There is a lot of pain when cultural, familial, or religious doctrines collide and conspire to prevent young people from being who they genuinely are. Tragically, sometimes the price people pay is ruinous and grave.

Numerous studies have shown that lesbian, gay, and bisexual youth have a higher rate of suicide attempts than do heterosexual youth. The Suicide Prevention Resource Center* synthesized these studies and

---

* Suicide Prevention Resource Center. (2008). Suicide risk and prevention for lesbian, gay, bisexual, and transgender youth. Newton, MA: Education Development Center, Inc.

estimated that between 30 and 40 percent of LGBT youth, depending on age and sex groups, have attempted suicide. Even as far back as 1988, there was research stating that between 30 and 40 percent of the young people who were attempting suicide were doing so because of sexual orientation confusion. It wasn't even that the young men and women were LGBT and felt frightened and confused; it was enough just to be questioning sexual orientation to lead them to despair; it was tragic when they felt they had nowhere to turn for support and help. That research was not allowed to be widely released, and a government document that explained it was pulled from distribution across the country for political reasons.

Such suicide rates among young men and women are unacceptable, and so is the fact that many LGBTQ kids take their own lives because of devastatingly hurtful rejection from their parents. This does not have to happen—we can change the homo-ignorance that still exists.

When it comes to LGBTQ issues, there are two terms that are often misunderstood. Even well-educated people use the terms "sexual orientation" and "sexual preference" interchangeably, and this is dangerously erroneous. Clarifying these two terms is an important first step in being able to discuss LGBTQ issues in a sensitive way. Sexual orientation is one's primary sexual arousal pattern over a period of time. We know that this is not a choice—no one wakes up one morning, looks out their window, and says, "Gee, what a nice day out there, I think I will be attracted to the same sex." Likewise, no one wakes up one morning, looks out their window, and says, "Gee, what a nice day out there, I think I will be attracted to the opposite sex." That simply doesn't happen. Sexual preference, however, is how you decide to act out your sexual orientation. This is a choice. Too many people end up being inauthentic to themselves by enacting a preference that differs from their orientation. People do this because society still has a heterosexual assumption—a heterosexual bias—that being heterosexual is somehow better, more acceptable, and healthier than being LGBTQ. Too many parents are not knowledgeable about these issues, so when their son or daughter does "come out" (a process by the way, and not an event) they don't know how to react.

Historically, fathers (and mothers) who learned about their son's or daughter's sexual orientation had very little actual information, and they ended up responding with biases they had been socially constructed to believe. These reactions can be devastating to young people as they struggle to know and accept themselves as fully-realized people—worthy of love and belonging—as well as proud and open about who they are. The importance of understanding the difference between sexual orientation and preference is significant; however, understanding the price people pay when culture pressures us to conform to biases and live incongruent and inauthentic lives . . . can be lifesaving.

***

It is difficult to comprehend how any parent could ever reject a child over something (like sexual orientation) that is not a choice. Considering Claire's mother's reaction to the news that her daughter is gay, Claire seems particularly lucky that her father responded the way that he did.

▶ Claire

"As soon as he said 'hello,' I started bawling. Then I told my dad through tears and gasps of breath that I had told Mom I wasn't straight and she didn't like me anymore. He asked if I wanted to come into Boston and have lunch with him. I caught the next train downtown, and when I got to South Station the first thing he said to me was, 'I'll never love you any less than before.' His kindness made me break down in tears again, and he told me that, although Mom probably wanted him to be yelling at me, he knew my life would be hard enough, and he didn't think I had done anything wrong. He genuinely wanted to know how I felt and whether being gay was a choice or not. He told me he'd work with my mother and said 'She'll get over it, just give her seventy . . . eighty years.'

I don't know what I would have done without my dad that day. I always knew that I had lucked out in the dad department, but I don't think I had ever felt so grateful for him being so understanding and compassionate. I would love for all men to be like that."

***

George stopped by my office the other day. He had watched the movie Milk, and he wanted to talk about how it affected him. George is a college senior and he is gay. As he talked about his new understanding of how one person (Harvey Milk) can clearly make a difference and how that inspires him, he mentioned how grateful he is to his own dad for his love and support. George said that his dad is one of his best friends.

▶ George

"According to the Oxford English Dictionary a dad is, 'one's father.' What does this even mean? A dad is so much more. He is not just a father: he is a hero, he is a friend, he is a mentor, he can be tough, he can be weak, he can be scary, he can be a fighter, and the most important thing is that he is unique.

My dad had parents who were not the most loving of parents. They did not show affection in any way and in some ways my dad was alone in the family. My grandparents loved each other a lot, and they sometimes excluded him from things. One of the saddest stories my dad ever told was that he was left by himself at Christmas when his parents went on a cruise. He said he had to make himself a TV dinner. I have never had to make myself a TV dinner for Christmas, I have never been alone on a holiday, and every night since I have been young we have said I love you before we go to bed. In fact, when I go home after being away for a long period of time, we have something called a family hug. The family hug has been a huge part of my family because it is a time for us to show how much we love each other.

The family hug I needed the most was on the night I came out. Coming out was the hardest and the easiest thing I have ever had to do. When I came out it was not really a shock to anyone. I still remember that November night. It would be a lie to say that when I came out they did cartwheels in the living room, but the first thing they did was to get up and come have a family hug. They will never know how much I needed that. I knew I was welcome, loved, and not alone. You often hear horror stories of men and women coming out and being ex-communicated by their families. They both said that they would love me no matter what.

Fast forward about a month later. My parents were driving me back up to St. Mike's for my first service trip. I was the happiest I have ever been. We were almost at school, and my dad said something that could have changed my relationship with him forever. My dad is a worrier, and he had this idea that I was going to get beat up for being gay. He was just concerned. He is my dad. Well, he said something along the lines of, 'George, maybe you have not met the right girl yet.' I remember telling him, 'Dad, I will love you always, but if you continue to think like that I will no longer be part of your life.' This was the only moment that my dad and I had an awkward bump in our relationship. I like to think that, when I came out, the watercolor painting my parents had melted away, and together we are painting a new one.

As we paint this new image together, I am very thankful for the relationship I have with them. My dad and my mom are very supportive of who I am. At first my dad, when he talked about me being gay would say, 'George's condition,' but he meant it in the most loving way. Knowing my dad and knowing he struggles with change, I knew he was trying, and I could not be happier. I know the first time I bring a guy home my dad is going to be the most awkward, loving, and caring dad a guy could ask for.

As I move forward and begin this new journey of adulthood I will always have the inspiration of my father. In many ways he has shown me to be always true to myself. Being a man is something that is different for all of us, and I think my dad understands that. He has never made me feel unmanly. Like every dad; every man is unique."

***

As Edward struggled to finally tell his father about his sexual identity, he feared that he was not going to "be the man" that his father wanted him to be. What then? What if he wasn't that man? What would happen to their relationship—to that bond between a father and a son? Let's see.

▶ Edward

"A man is someone who has a passion for sports. While I was growing up, my dad and I would always watch football games together and go to baseball games at Fenway. Although I have not become a sports enthusiast like my dad, being interested in sports has always been part of my vision of what a man is supposed to be like. When I was younger, I played football for a short period of time, which was something that my dad always wanted me to do. Later, I participated in sports that were not traditionally 'macho'—I played volleyball and did gymnastics—and my father always encouraged me to do the best I could.

I think my vision of what it means to be a man changed about halfway through my life, when I came out as a gay man. My father was the last person I came out to. I was scared of what his reaction was going to be, and I did not feel like I was being the man he wanted me to be. I can still remember coming out to him, having him sit down next to my bed and cry when I told him. His reaction shocked me at first; I didn't understand why he was crying, but then he explained that it was because he wanted grandchildren. Later, I assured him that this is still a possibility. After it sunk in a bit, he told me that no matter what, he would always love me; he was not angry; he did not reject me; and he accepted me for who I am. This showed me that no matter what, a real man will love his children and accept them for who they are.

After I came out, my dad had less of an influence on my vision of a man. I think this was because I felt like I was redefining what kind of a man I was going to be. I was searching for answers to questions about my identity that my father could not answer. At this point I began to look to older gay men to figure out how to navigate this new world. This is not to say that my father did not influence me; he influenced the most important aspects of my vision of masculinity, laying out for me the foundation of what a real man should be. But I had to alter that vision slightly to incorporate this new aspect of myself. The things I learned from my father about being a man did not change; I was just seeing them from a different perspective. The thing I had to take into account was that some people don't see gay men as real men, but I know that I am still a real man, and I thank my father for instilling this confidence in me."

***

I was intrigued by Fred's image of what a man is, which he explains separately from how his father influenced him. It is interesting to see how society has influenced him.

▶ Fred

"For all of my life, or at least the parts that I can remember, I have been inundated with ideas of what I should be like as a man. From the TV shows, cartoons, and movies that I watched growing up, to interactions with my friends and peers, and even from adults, I have been given a message of what I should be like as I grew and developed into a man. Some of those traits included being strong, athletic, playing sports, being straight, not showing emotion, being tough, having a good sense of humor, earning average grades, and being popular with the opposite sex. These were just some of the major traits that were communicated to me and defined what I perceived to be as the definition of a man. However, even with all of the explicit and implicit messages, my father was the one who had the most influence on the man that I was to become.

Before I can even discuss my father and his influences on me, the question of 'what is a man' must be addressed. In my own personal opinion, a man is a person with a penis. In addition to that important fact, a man is someone who is compassionate toward his significant other and his family (including children), has a strong understanding of himself, and is comfortable with who he is. He is compassionate, patient, understanding, has a strong work ethic, is a role model for his children and others, and is able to make sacrifices, both personal and beyond, to help out those he cares about. This may be a surprising definition—many would view my definition as soft, or as describing a 'girly-man.' But I believe that being a man in today's world is not about how strong you are, how many women you can get, how degrading you can be toward the opposite sex through words or actions, how much beer you can drink, or any other stereotypical characteristic.

As I graduated from high school and went on to college, my father continued to influence me. He continues to set an example of supporting, caring, and being a strong role model for me. It was in my first year of college that I came out, and it was my first weekend home from college when I told my parents that I was gay. This was not an easy task, but my parents were extremely supportive and so was the rest of my family. (Although I later found out that my dad thought I was going to tell them that I got someone pregnant.) Even when he heard that I was gay, my father told me how he and my mother had unconditional love for me; that no matter what, they loved me for being me. There is a taboo about gay men because of what our culture says how men should be. So for my father to accept me and still love me was huge. There is no greater feeling than hearing those words from your role model and largest masculine influence in your life. It was a very meaningful event in my life to have my parents love and support the person that I am."

Chapter 6

Wonderful Fathers

In hundreds of subtle ways, our culture suggests how fathers and sons are supposed to interact as "real" men. Unfortunately, many of these messages are damaging. For example, I recently saw an advertisement for a high-end smartphone. In it are two men acting as father and son who are looking at phones in a store and speaking in an abbreviated code that is meant, apparently, to mimic the truncated speech patterns of texting. Their conversation has to be translated by subtitles at the bottom of the screen because it is practically monosyllabic. In this bizarre code, the father tells the son that he is proud of him and that he will miss him when he is away at college. Instead of having these two men engage in an open, emotional dialogue—as is the case in a similar commercial featuring a mother and daughter—the men talk in code. The emotion of the father-son bond is twice-removed: first by their avoidance of meaningful verbal interaction with each other, and second, by the assumed complicity of the audience. We are shown a stereotype of male emotional response—that to show emotion is embarrassing and somehow, taboo—and in order to "get" the joke, we have to buy into the idea that all men are unable to communicate emotion. This type of stereotypical behavior, when in the hands of marketing folks, helps to enforce visions of masculinity and fatherhood that can hurt sons and daughters for generations. Fortunately, the essays in this chapter show us that this doesn't have to be so. Many of my students write very lovingly about their fathers and are happy with and proud of these positive, close relationships; however, and ironically, they consider their dads quite unique and "different" from most of their friends' fathers.

***

Peg's father has challenged gender role stereotypes. Appreciating his example, Peg tells us that she compares other males in her life to her father and "pushes them to acquire the qualities my father puts forth." She is finishing her master's degree in counseling. I recently had lunch with Peg and her boyfriend and could see that he does indeed seem to reflect many of the values Peg credits her dad with instilling in her.

▶ Peg

"It is through the example of my father that I have been able to construct an idea of what a man is, and I believe this man has a lot to offer others—even if he doesn't fit in with society's idea of masculinity.

When I was six years old, my parents decided to follow through with a divorce after numerous attempts to make it work. These attempts were mostly sought by my father, in the hope that he could salvage the relationship and maintain a level of normalcy for my brother and me. While my parents went through the divorce process, my father rented an apartment in the building where he has his chiropractic office. Every weekend, my brother and I spent time with my dad. Some days we would go to breakfast at Friendly's and other days we would just enjoy each other's company. As the custody battle began to unfold, my dad spoke with his lawyer about his chances. His lawyer turned to him and said, 'Well, that just doesn't happen.' My dad refused to accept this answer. His lawyer explained that it would be a tough battle and he would need to provide evidence of why my mother was unfit to receive custody. My dad was able to make a case against my mom, who soon decided it was unnecessary to continue, leaving my brother and me to be raised by my father.

My dad faced many struggles in his efforts to receive custody of my brother and me. When he finally was granted custody of us, the battle was not over. People did not believe he would be able to handle being the father and the mother. My dad managed to continue the balancing act to provide for our family. He was also willing to acknowledge that he wasn't perfect. He didn't get these roles right every time, but he was determined to find a way to make it work. On a typical day, my dad would have office hours from nine to five and a lunch break that was usually spent picking my brother and me up from school. After he returned home from work, he cooked dinner and helped us with homework, which included anything from checking it over to full-blown study sessions. After we finished our homework and went to bed, my dad worked on office notes, billing, and paperwork. On an average day, my dad was in bed by two in the morning and up again by five to start it all over. As we got older, we were able to take on more responsibility to help alleviate some of the stressors in his life. However, my dad still embodies the roles of breadwinner and housewife to this day. My dad has worked to break down the societal gender boundaries about what a 'man' is capable of in regards to career and home life.

My dad has also shown me how a 'real man' asks for help. To make sure he was providing my brother and me with the best life he could, my dad reached out to family and friends to help him. He was able to rely on people to care for my brother and me after school and provide us with opportunities to socialize. My dad was also 'man enough' to ask for financial help from my family when he needed it. He didn't let his pride get in the way of providing a happy and healthy childhood for his children. His willingness to lean on others around him in times of need is admirable and I feel that it contributes to my idea of how a 'real man' behaves.

The important thing I try to remember is that my father wasn't forced to take on any of the responsibilities he had. He could have left us with my mom and visited us when he got a chance. Instead, he went after this life and was willing to sacrifice everything, from friends to wealth, to provide for his family. That sacrifice is something that is commendable. My dad was willing to give up the future he saw for himself to provide an even brighter future for my brother and me. Sacrifice is only part of the equation. My view of a man has been influenced by a male figure who refuses to be in accordance with the societal view. A man must be willing to be emotionally vulnerable. He must be sensitive and caring. A man values his family. A man steps up to challenges and takes responsibility. A man should be willing to take on the challenges life puts in front of him. A man also should know when he needs help, and he shouldn't be afraid to ask for it. A man understands perfection does not exist and accepts failures as learning opportunities.

In these few simple examples I have been able to demonstrate how my father influenced my idea of what a 'man' is and does. My father was willing to break down boundaries in an effort to have a happy life. He did not let his pride get in the way of achieving the life he wanted for himself or his children. My father is my role model and I continuously strive for this in the males I have in my life. I push them to acquire the qualities my father puts forth. Witnessing these qualities has made me a better person and I can only hope others have been influenced by his character to make life changes for themselves."

Brent raises an issue in the following essay about derogatory, sexist, or violent comments about women and reflects on how much those kinds of statements disturb him. In workshops or classes with young men, I often ask, "How would you feel if your mother, your sister, your grandmother, your girlfriend or any female friend were to hear you speaking like that?" The emotion behind their answers is often overwhelming. As Brent shows us, violence doesn't have to be physical, and how our fathers respond provides us with a crucial model of how or how not to be.

▶ Brent

"Growing up in a male-dominated family has shaped the way I view and treat women. It wasn't until I started this class that I realized that my upbringing really influenced how I see certain relationships in my life. I am the youngest of three sons and a cousin to a family of five boys; much of my life has been surrounded by testosterone, sports, and all things 'male.' Aside from all the masculine influences, I've reached a point in my life where I can appreciate the role that my younger sister has played in my understanding and respect for women, as well.

My parents were by no means strict when I was younger, but they had their rules. My brothers and I would wrestle and fight, but we weren't allowed to get out of control, and we were never allowed to have toy guns or play *Grand Theft Auto*. Rules like these made for some difficult times with my peers—they thought I was a "loser" for not having those violent games. Looking back, I think it was very important that my parents instilled in us that violent behaviors are unnecessary and wrong.

Following my parents' rules helped to shape me, but nothing they ever told me played a larger role in who I am today than the unspoken messages from my father. I can honestly say that I have never witnessed my parents in a fight. They may have their disagreements every once in a while, but it's never more than just that—a disagreement. They've always been able to work out disagreements in a calm and rational manner. I think this comes not only from the love they have for each other but the amount of respect they have for each other. In the book *The Macho Paradox*, Jackson Katz speaks about fathers and their relationships with women. One passage really jumped out at me because it illustrates exactly what my father has done so well:

'Clearly one of the most important roles a father or a father figure can play in his son's life is to teach by example. If men are always respectful toward women and never verbally abuse them, their sons in all likelihood will learn to be similarly respectful. Nonetheless every man who has a son should be constantly aware that how he treats women is not just between him and the women—there is a little set of eyes that is always watching him and picking up cues about how a man is supposed to act.'

My own father rarely made overt comments about condemning violence against women, but he never hit, screamed at, or made inappropriate comments to my mother, and this is something that has definitely been embedded in my mind and my brothers'. (I have observed many of my brothers' relationships with women throughout their lives as well, and it is obvious in all of them the amount of respect they have for their significant others.)

My extended family tended to be a little different, but the lessons I took away from those relationships are just as valuable. I was lucky enough to grow up with two sets of grandparents. My father's parents were similar to my parents in that I can't remember them fighting, and my grandfather was always gracious and courteous to my grandmother. He was an extremely hard worker and valued his family much like my father does. My mother's parents don't exactly have the same type of relationship, but they still show a great amount of love and care for the rest of the family. Her father is often very disrespectful to my grandmother and doesn't think he does anything wrong. I was able to see firsthand how hurtful that type of behavior was. The positive side of this is that my parents always told us that this was wrong and never to treat women like he does. My father will not speak to that grandfather anymore because of some of his actions. I hate the hostility, but my father is sending the right message by standing up to him and telling him that his behavior is unacceptable."

***

I have had the opportunity to teach all four of the siblings from Brent's family (three young men and a young woman). Sharon is Brent's sister. It is fascinating to see the same dad from the perspective of each of his children. These siblings didn't hesitate to share their views about their dad. The role their mom played in their upbringing is also evident and something that many, many of my students included in their essays—perhaps someday I will write a book on how mothers influenced our views of what a man is!

▶ **Sharon**

"Let me preface by saying I have lived an extremely privileged life thanks to my amazing parents and brothers. My father has set the bar very high for my expectations of what a man is supposed to be like. However, it does not seem right to talk about my dad without first briefly writing about my mother and their relationship. My parents started dating when they were fourteen years old. They never took a break, and despite doubts from some family members who were originally upset that their Irish-Catholic son was dating a Jewish girl, my parents were married after completing college. Of course, they get angry or annoyed with one another from time to time, but I do not think that they have ever gotten into a yelling argument. They actually still *flirt*, which, while making me incredibly uncomfortable, makes me feel equally happy because I can say my parents are still totally in love.

My dad and I have a really fun relationship. We tease my mom together, watch our shows together, and communicate on a regular basis—even if sometimes it is just through text or email. This fun relationship does not always result in serious conversations between the two of us, which I am fine with because my mom and I can have serious conversations more comfortably. He lets her handle talking to me about any issues I may run into, probably because he does not want to hear about any of my relationships with guys. However, I still know that I could always go to him if need be.

Being the youngest child and the only girl in my family, my parents and brothers have always spoiled me; I always have been and always will be 'Daddy's princess.' On weekends, the minute I woke up I would run into my parents' bed and watch TV with them, cuddling with my dad when I am sure all he wanted to do was sleep. On school days, my dad would wake me up, make me breakfast (heart shaped pancakes on special days), then walk me to the end of our short driveway to wait for the bus with me, often kicking a soccer ball around while we waited. When I got older, I became a bit of a brat and was embarrassed by him waiting for the bus so I asked him to stop. After that, he would always be watching out the window to see me off. It was not until pretty recently that I realized he watched because waiting for the bus with me had been a highlight of his days and he realized that those days were winding down. Hiding behind the curtain watching me get on the bus was his way of cherishing every moment. My dad is sensitive and gives his whole heart to others, and because of his example, I expect all men to be the same. Yet my expectations often seem to be too high.

I hear many people say, 'I've only seen my dad cry once.' That's too bad. My dad cries openly, quite often. It pains me every time, but it is one of his traits that I really value because he does show emotion. Every time I leave to come back to Saint Michael's he tears up; this serves as a constant reminder of how important I am to him. Recently, I sent my family a link asking them to please donate to help a classmate who needs to raise over nine thousand dollars for a new service dog. My dad responded immediately, admitting the story made him cry and asked if he could forward my message to all of his contacts as well as if he could contact the young man directly. It is this genuine kindness and caring for others that I admire in my father. I believe that only very special men exhibit such traits.

In addition to being sensitive and caring, my dad is also very skilled in many areas. He can build and repair just about anything. At our lake house in Maine, he built the deck; he did much of the electrical work; he installed interior woodwork; and he can even fix plumbing problems. His handiwork does not stop at homeownership, though, as he can also fix, install, and repair a lot of issues in our cars. My dad's vast knowledge of so many things involving manual labor astonishes me. I get the sense that many young men these days are not as knowledgeable or skillful in home or car care, and because of my dad, my vision of a man includes being someone who can fix little things around the house and doesn't have to call a repairperson for everything.

While I have realized over the years that I hold men to extremely high standards, I cannot seem to change my vision of what a man should be. My dad can do little wrong in my eyes and for that, I envision a man as being just like him: funny, sensitive, loving unconditionally, yet strong and skilled—just like he is. This is my vision of the perfect man. Hopefully, as I continue to grow and mature, I will lower my standards and adjust my vision of how a man should be to better my relationships and not expect too much of people."

***

Laura seems to have a clear, healthy understanding of her father's abilities and the way he differs from other dads. As she compares him to other fathers, they are the outliers and he is the one she respects.

▶ Laura

"Mom was always working, but so was Dad. I never realized the role my father held in my family until I looked at the dynamics of my best friend's family. Her father traveled around the world every few weeks, leaving his wife with all the responsibilities; in contrast, my dad and mom carried equal weight in our upbringing. Dad worked the usual nine-to-five until I was in middle school. During that time, Mom was per-diem—she would be the one to greet us getting off the bus, and Dad would be the one who spent all night and weekend playing with us. I never saw Dad's work to be problematic because he made the extra effort to coach our teams, teach our religious education classes, come to school events, and sing with my sister and me at bedtime. He put 110 percent into our family, and that took quite a bit of balance—I now realize not all dads can do. I was blessed.

I had a definitive picture of my father being the sensitive father who would play dress-up with me or would cover my paper route for me early on a Sunday when he did not want me on my bike in the snow. As the years have progressed, however, this image of my father has been challenged. As time went on, I realized Dad had been living with lots of financial stress that he had hidden in order to make us all believe that things were okay.

When I reflect on the role Dad has played in my life, I realize he formed my expectations of how all men should be. When I interact with other fathers, I find myself comparing them regularly to Dad. I cringe seeing fathers doing the stereotypical 'male fun' things like wrestling, poking fun at the child, or ignoring the child. The athletic father of an upper class family I babysat for found no problem with telling his kid he was a loser or lame for choosing to do an arts and crafts project with me or for opting to cook versus play football outside. Because I constantly compare everyone to my dad, I see situations like this one as unnecessary and debilitating for the child. My dad's approach seems ideal and he certainly was not always perfect with it, but he attempted to be grounded in what he believed on how to raise us. In my eyes, it comes down to honesty, sensitivity, a listening ear, and patience. When these aspects of a father are lacking, the child and the child's behavior eventually suffer."

***

Tom's feelings about his father have changed over the years from embarrassment to admiration. He mentions the "overly macho" image that society presents us of men and then describes the ways his own dad doesn't match that image. As it turns out, the bond he and his dad have forged is one that Tom cherishes, and it has clearly shaped the type of man he has become.

▶ Tom

"My vision of what a man is supposed to be has really been constructed by my father. He is a family man first and foremost. His role in our family is clearly at the head of the table, but that is not to say that he and my mother do not share every duty. They both cook, clean, and provide for us. My dad does not take the 'alpha male' role in our family; he is more of an equal with my mom, but his authoritative line is firmly drawn.

I once looked at my father as an example of what I did not want to be. I wanted to be my own person. I tried so hard for so long to be different from him—not because he is a bad man, but because I always considered him to be so lame. When we're young we always think that we are so much cooler than we actually are, and in our eyes our parents are the opposite of cool. So, like any adolescent, I attempted to separate myself from my father in fields such as appearance, actions, and personality. However, gradually I have become a sort of clone of him; so much of his style and presence has influenced me. As I matured, I realized that I was inevitably becoming him and I felt good about that.

I find myself envying parts of his fashion sense, for example, that I had once thought were his least favorable attributes. Being raised as a fisherman, he naturally wore boat shoes and when I was younger I hated them. As I matured I found myself loving them. I wear them almost every day and have actually influenced my friends to wear them. When I was in prep school, my teammates called my dad 'The Fonz' (after Arthur Fonzarelli from *Happy*

Days) due to the fact that he would wear a leather jacket and scarf to my hockey games. While I hope I never wear a leather jacket, I like wearing scarves in the winter. When my dad coached me in Little League, he used to wear tank tops and my mother would give him a hard time because she thought he looked horrible. At the time, I felt somewhat embarrassed. But I grew to realize that so much of what he wore (such as the tank tops) were a part of his fisherman/beach bum persona. This style wore off on me over time, and I'm sure some people think I look as ridiculous as I thought my father did.

There is a part of me that I adopted from my mother, this is my crazy wild side; my reserved side, I got from my father. Sometimes he does not need words to express himself. I can recall hockey trips we took all over the northeast when we would have to drive for hours on end. On those car rides we did not need to learn each other's life stories and he did not need to teach me life lessons; we would talk sometimes, but at times there would be nothing but silence. Each other's company was enough and we still share moments when we are able to soak in the moment with no word exchange. This type of communication cannot be used with everyone; it takes two comparable people to share such quiet moments. It is a sort of male-bonding that I can share with my father and some of my friends.

With everything my father and I have been through together, it is still difficult to put into words exactly what he means to me and what he has taught me about what it means to be a man. I guess it all comes down to love and caring and being able to convey that to others. I have always been very open with my feelings, and I owe a lot of that to my father. His openness with me allowed me to feel comfortable with myself and with my love for others, and I am blessed with the ability to show this. Growing up, I never had any doubt that he loved our family and me and this is important.

Young men today are taught to be overly masculine and to exert power and control, striking fear into the hearts of their peers. However, a real man is one who can have love in his heart and can show it openly—eliminating hate from his life. Once we eliminate the overly macho image that America has become infatuated with, we can also alleviate the hate and power obsession that goes along with it.

My father is generally the opposite of the violent, 'alpha male' image. He is balding, has small hands, cooks, cleans, wears sweaters, and wears glasses when he reads. He drinks low calorie beer and orders salads when we go out to eat. He drives the speed limit in a modest sedan, tells me he loves me, and gives me hugs. We own a piece of shit TV and have two fat cats. He works out on an elliptical machine, speaks softly, and doesn't wear deodorant. He defies the male image that we have been taught to admire and fear at the same time. It is his influence and image that have shown me what it really means to be a man. To love and to care is divine: a peaceful existence wherein we admire and cherish the things we love will provide us with the life we are searching for. I have discovered this indirectly through the lessons my father has taught me."

***

It is interesting to see that Molly has such a clear picture of her father and how his behaviors over her lifetime have shaped her views on men, and how, as she states in her last sentence, "I'd be thrilled to find a man as great as my Pops." Although many students in earlier chapters might have wanted a different kind of a father and male role model, many other students do feel as Molly does and want to find someone just like their Dad.

▶ **Molly**

"I call my dad 'Pops,' and the way I see it, it's kind of like that cereal commercial with the jingle that goes, 'I've gotta have my pops.' Everybody has his or her own view, perhaps even stereotype, of what a man is: strong, too tough to show emotion, hardworking, brave, athletic, etc. Rarely are words like compassionate, caring, or loving ever associated with men. I'm proud to say, however, that my father has showed me that a true man can be all those things and more. Humorous, sentimental, humble, dedicated, open-minded, intelligent, strong, courageous, sincere, hardworking, and loving are just a few of the characteristics that I would use to describe what a man is, and that is all thanks to my father.

Growing up in a family with three brothers, it's safe to say that I'm a 'daddy's girl' through and through. As you can imagine, 'boy time' was common in our household. Two-versus-two touch football games, playing catch in the yard, and discussing game strategies at the dinner table were common activities. Sports and competition have always been valued in our house and I would pester my brothers to no end to let me play catch. But the more I matured, the more I realized that sometimes guys just need to be guys. It's not that my father didn't care about my athletics (in fact, he attended just about every gymnastics meet I've ever had and sat through endless dance recitals); rather, he could relate more to the sports my brothers were involved in and there is nothing wrong with that. Watching the Patriots play on Sunday afternoons and gathering for poker night with the neighborhood guys is what men do. It doesn't mean that girls can't participate, it's just that a man values the times when he can let loose, talk about 'guy things' and get a break from his occasionally nagging wife. That's just the way a man works.

However, father/daughter time has included some of the most cherished moments of my life. It seems silly, but the day I won the 'artist of the week' contest in the third grade, my dad made plans to pick me up early from school and spend the afternoon enjoying a perfect lunch at McDonald's. He was really busy at work during this time, but he made sure to drop everything to make this day happen. I don't think he has ever realized how much this meant to me, but that's just it, he's never needed to receive constant praise. I guess you can say this trait forms my idea of the best kind of man: not arrogant or in need of credit, just modest.

When you do someone a favor, more often than not you want or expect something in return. This has never been the case for my father. His genuinely humble nature has shaped him into the successful and well-respected man that he is. He is always willing to go the extra mile to help someone in need but never expects anything back. Whether it's that moment when I get into my car dreading to look at the low fuel light blinking in my face, but the tank has miraculously been filled, or still tipping the waitress more than 20 percent even after she spilled two full soda glasses on his lap, my dad's subtle gestures can turn anyone's day around. In addition, it's a true man who is willing enough to step outside his comfort zone for the benefit of another. Just this past December, my father reminded me of this characteristic by accepting the task of volunteering at a homeless shelter in Boston on Christmas Eve. It reminded me of the potential every man has to make a difference in the world. Although my father may not believe it, he has made a true difference in the lives of many.

He has also taught me that a man should take initiative and value respect. He is one of the hardest-working men I have ever known. I have decided that a man should be strong enough to endure a life of physical labor, but still keep enough energy to play with his kids—and that is exactly how my father lives. My dad chose not to go to college, but to start a family and business instead. Academics were never pushed too hard on us as kids; instead, we valued effort and commitment. I had friends whose parents would ground them for a bad grade on a report card, but my parents never did. In fact, I can't recall many times when my father even raised his voice. It takes a lot to upset my dad. He never shows anger, just disappointment. Because of this, I have learned that real men don't need to yell or fight to show their power; they can express concern in a calm, collected fashion that gets the point across just as clearly.

Also, contrary to popular belief, a man does have the ability to listen. My father listens, and although sometimes his 'selective hearing' gets the best of him, he pays attention when it matters most. The advice that follows is straight from the heart. If the advice can't be formed, the support still remains. A year ago on Valentine's Day, I set off for a six-month adventure to the other side of the world. It was my mother who cried in my arms as I said goodbye, while my dad held himself together. It wasn't until I boarded the plane and opened up the envelope my mother had sent with me that I discovered my father's unique way of expression. While my mother wrote a four page letter, my father kept it simple, as men do: 'Roses are red, your bedroom dark blue…' As I continued reading, my heart melted. It was a simple ten lines that truly hit home. His witty humor, sincere love, and talent for writing shined. '… I love you so much, don't drink too much hops, and remember you can always call me your pops.' We've always said my father is a 'man of few words,' but this poem served as the most genuine reminder that real men can rhyme and aren't too tough to show it.

We have a little personal contest going too; every time we make a phone call to each other, we joke about how long it lasts. I think our personal best is up to thirty-two minutes. The point I'm trying to make is that even though a man sometimes may not act as if he cares, my father has proven to me in more ways than one that they actually do. Sometimes men just have a hard time expressing themselves, but if you give them a chance, once they feel comfortable enough, they truly can open up.

I've learned that it's okay for a man to cry, but if they don't it doesn't mean that they are like the Tin Man and missing a heart. I can count on one hand the number of times I've seen my father cry, but one of those times has been the most memorable moment to shape my view of how a true man should act. My mother and I were about to board our flight to visit some schools down south when we got the call that one of my best friends and her sister were killed that morning in a car accident. I felt empty. It wasn't until my father picked us up from the airport and held me in his arms that I felt a smidgen of life flow back into me. Having his strong arms wrapped around me radiated this incredible sense of comfort and safety and as I looked up into his eyes and saw their glossy teardrop coating, I was reminded of how lucky I was to be his daughter. It was in this moment that I realized how much I wish every man could be like my father: strong enough and brave enough to make me feel safe and whole in the hardest situation I have ever faced in my life.

It's interesting to see the way my dad views a man in comparison to the way he has formulated my view of one. He has always told me to make sure I 'don't just settle,' and that the man I end up dating (God willing) 'knows how to throw a football.' This simple statement has become quite a joke between my father and me, but the more I think about it, the more I realize how telling it is. It is a pure example of how strongly my father values his goals in creating the best life he can for his family, and yes, he has done just that. Research has shown that women typically end up marrying someone similar to their own father, and well, if that's the case, I'd be thrilled to find a man as great as my Pops."

***

Nancy challenges what she has seen and read about fathers; she has developed her own view of fathers because of her dad. She makes some interesting assumptions regarding the stereotypes she has about masculinity and how her father doesn't fit them. I wonder how she felt when she was younger and compared him to the fathers of her friends. She definitely loves and admires him, and she also knows that he is not like other fathers.

▶ Nancy

"Ever since I can remember, my father has been a hero and a true man in my eyes. My dad does not fit into the historical gender role of a husband and a father. Some people may disagree with me and I may sound biased, but my father is the kindest, most intelligent, loyal, faithful, *real* man I know. My father is not your average man. He's not obsessed with sports, he doesn't drive a slick car, and he definitely cannot fix anything. In fact, he is a lot different from your average man. He loves to read philosophy, he has a knack for teaching himself languages (he speaks six fluently), he likes to clean, he likes to garden and loved to travel in Europe. (He has also run marathons and climbed mountains, including Mt. Kilimanjaro in Africa.)

My parents both work full-time, outside the home. Both are very involved in their professions and seem to enjoy their jobs. In addition to their full-time jobs, I have seen them both working at home, co-managing the house, and taking care of me. My dad shops for food, cleans, and does the 'heavy lifting.' He can even cook when necessary, although he is not a gourmet chef.

Unlike a lot of dads I know, he has always been involved not only in running our home, but also in taking care of me. (Because of the demands of my mother's profession, my dad took on some 'mothering' responsibilities as well. I think a true man provides for his family by doing whatever is required, regardless of traditional gender roles.) My dad would take me to pre-school and regular school every morning before he went to work. Later, he would be back to pick me up in the early evening after soccer, ski team, or swim practice. On the weekends, he would always have time to drive my girlfriends and me to the movies or the mall. He would play with me a lot on the weekends. My mom's work often prevented her from coming with us, but my dad was really happy to spend all that extra time with me.

Except for the separate assignments of 'heavy lifting' and gourmet cooking, my dad and mom both easily did their jobs with no noticeable gender stereotyping. Each could do almost any job required. The model for me has been one of collaboration and cooperation, with man and a woman comfortable performing essential work and childcare in the home. I don't really know another way, so I will assume that I will have this kind of relationship with my future husband.

What I know to be true about men via my dad's example is often at odds with what I see in the movies or on TV, as well as with what I read in books. In the media, men are often portrayed as emotionally clueless, controlling of women, and physically intimidating, yet often dependent on their wives, girlfriends, and mothers. Sometimes they are portrayed as emotionally sensitive and supportive, but not too often. Sometimes men in some other cultures are depicted as the 'leaders' in both their public and private lives, behaving the same way in both spheres, remote from the emotional needs of their families.

My dad is definitely not like that. He is very loving and caring and sensitive. My earliest memories are of a man with a sweet and kind nature, who was thrilled to have a little girl. All my life, he has been consistently available to me, always willing to talk to me and to help me. He is not judgmental or bossy. He does not try to control me or to minimize me because I am his child, or a female child. If my dad sounds too good to be true, I guess he is.

He did not have a father himself, having lost his father when he was three year old. While he was primarily raised by his mother, his uncle was involved with him as a sort of father-figure. My dad's uncle was basically a sweet and kind man too. So I guess that my dad took after him. I feel that I am the beneficiary of many of my dad's dreams. I feel his commitment and I follow his guidance. I know that he wants things for me that he never had. Many dads want the same things for their children, but can't show it very well. My dad is not afraid to show his feeling and even admit when he has made a mistake. So I have the best of all worlds: a father who is devoted and father who can show his feelings and talk to me.

I think that a girl's relationship with her father is the most influential of all her relationships with men. He is the template by which she will compare, consciously and unconsciously, all other men. Psychologically, we carry our parents inside ourselves, even if they are not present. So this assignment was an important one because it made me think about not only how my dad is in reality, but also about my image of him, of the first man I have known, deep inside me, in my mind and in my heart. This is lucky for me in my life, because I think that it is unlikely that I will marry, date, or even tolerate an abusive and devaluing man. If men don't talk and show me that they are decent and caring, hopefully I will not be interested in pursuing any kind of a relationship with the. Having a dad like mine is like being vaccinated against troublesome men.

So what is a man to me? A man is someone who is loyal to his wife and children. He helps to support them, not just financially but also emotionally. He takes an active role in child rearing and in running the home. He values education and a spiritual life. A man stands for strong values. You can count on him. My father has taught me that a true man is someone who is kind-hearted, not the head honcho. Loving. Involved. Helping. Loyal. Although I did not think the same way when I was younger, I now know if I ever had a problem, no matter how personal, I could always talk to my dad. Even if it was 2 am."

***

Here is Ken's story of how he was "fathered" by a grandmother and how he is supported by her love and understanding. In addition to fathers, mothers and grandparents have a role to play in constructing our view of a man. Ken's survival certainly would have been very different had it not been for his grandmother, who was also clearly influenced by her father. It is interesting to note the implicit messages about masculinity that Ken has absorbed: namely, that being "in charge" is a masculine trait.

▶ Ken

"My childhood was unconventional to say the least. By the time I was two years old, my mother had passed away and my father was no longer a part of my life. My father was a man I know little about. As I've been told, it all began in the summer of 1987; a Martha's Vineyard romance that quickly turned into marriage. Knowing little about this man, my mother's family was hesitant to allow the marriage to take place, but he got his way. He was 6-foot-4, very muscular, and had the people skills of a politician. Apparently, my father was able to win everyone over with the snap of his fingers, and he took full advantage of that when it came to my mother. After four years of marriage and a two-year-old child, my father left us—leaving my mother heartbroken and inconsolable. He found another woman and was in love with her. Shortly after my father broke the news, my mother passed away in a car accident. While the police report claimed there was no sign of suicide, the thought has always crossed my mind and I have placed a certain amount of blame on my father for her death.

After the accident, I spent several months classified as a ward of the state, and while I never lived in foster care protection, my family was unsure of what to do with me. Once things settled down, my father, on the advice of his lawyers, gave custody of me to my grandmother. At the age of forty-eight, after burying her first daughter, my grandmother gave up her aspirations of retirement and decided to raise me. She had been through a woman's worst nightmares—infidelity, divorce, death, and more. Yet despite her hardships, she remained strong and continued to be the patriarch of the entire family. This is the story of my grandmother who continues to work hard to be the mother, father, and grandmother in my life, so that I never have to feel the pain of being different.

While the assignment question was 'How did your father socially construct your vision of what a man is or what a man is supposed to be?' I chose to write how my grandmother, to the best of her ability, 'socially constructed' my vision of what it is to be a man. More importantly, she taught me how to be a good person and a respectable member of society. I had to figure out other things on my own. How to mow a lawn or use different tools was all done by trial and error, and I'm pleased to say I'm successful at both. My 'father' is unconventional, but hey, as a twenty-two-year-old gay man, many think I, too, am unconventional. Many have asked if I think I'm gay because of my upbringing or I hear the sympathy from others saying, 'Poor Ken, if only he had a father.' Well, I do have a father. I have a father and mother all wrapped up into an amazing woman—my grandmother. Without her and her strength, I would not be the man I am today."

***

Time and time again my male students have made the following comment as they end their papers (as Will does): "I can only hope that I will be as good a man." While touching, this sentiment is also troubling: These students are assuming that they are not already a "good man" or "as good a man" as their fathers. I always write many, many comments on my students' papers in order to raise questions, probe for their critical thinking, and ask if they have ever shared their thoughts with their mother or fathers. One of the comments I most often make when I read "I can only hope that I will be as good a man" is this: "What makes you think you aren't already?" Will credits his father with allowing him to form his own model of masculinity, and it looks like he has done a very fine job.

▶ **Will**

Throughout my growth as an individual, my father has socially constructed my view of a man in such a way that I could think for myself and form my own model of what I think a man is and should be. Never at any time did my father stress a specific example and tell me, 'This is what a man is.' Instead, he would consistently bring out the best in the people around him, hence creating positive examples for me to observe and learn from. At twenty-four, my vision of what a man should be is best represented through the examples my father has inadvertently presented, both positive and negative. Most importantly, I have been able to construct this understanding through observing my father's actions and listening to his exchanges with people.

My impression of a real man is a person who is modest, patient, and trusted. A man is also honest and respectful toward his family and peers, and he is committed to helping not only the people around him, but also those at a distance as well – through financial assistance when physical help is not possible.

My father started his own residential construction business in Vermont when he was twenty-one years old. With no college education and limited management experience, he started and ran his company for over twenty-five years. I have countless memories of my father owning and operating his own company. For those twenty-plus years, my father woke up at 5 am every morning with his nose to the grindstone. On the weekends, I was fortunate enough to witness my father work and earn a living. I saw him interact with his employees and small business partners, and I never saw him hesitate to jump in the construction hole and help the laborers when assistance was needed. My father never had the attitude that he was 'the boss man,' separate from his workers. He was one of them—thus his humility. Through his hardworking and determined nature, I saw my father build trustworthy relationships with every person he worked with. Everyone who knew my dad or was involved in the construction business knew he was trustworthy, loyal, and extremely hardworking. These traits embody my understanding of what a man is and should be.

Growing up, I quickly developed a very active and competitive nature. At an early age, athletics became a very important part of my life. I played hockey, soccer, lacrosse, and my never-quit attitude allowed me to pick up any sport I wanted. Aside from choosing hockey because I loved playing the game myself, my father's love of hockey played a substantial role in my affinity for it. I watched my father play like a gentleman, and learned that the real triumph of the game was, and is, a game well played with fellow athletes and not foes. I played to win but not to hurt, and the game was over when the scoreboard reflected that. My father was never one to bring the negative home but he also never hesitated to teach from moments he saw as remarkable.

My father coached me all through youth hockey and high school. Everything I learned about the game through my father was essentially an analogy of life and a direction of how I should act as a man. My father always told me to skate and practice hard; to play with knowledge and humility; and to treat fellow athletes with respect regardless of their temperament. Modesty and a respect of the game were emphasized repeatedly. I was able to extract those traits from a game like hockey and put them to work in a model of what I believe a 'real' man is.

More important than any business transaction or relationship made in the business world was my father's commitment to my personal growth as well as the rest of the family. Nothing was, or still is, more important than the well-being and direction of each member of the family. How my father handled family life provided me with a plethora of experiences that allowed me to construct my vision of a man with integrity. His treatment of all women, not only my mother and sister, sends a message to me that women are equal to men and not simply objects. His straightforwardness and self-control with family matters gave me a great idea of how a man should act around his family and peers. Quite obviously, my father has been a remarkable influence on my understanding on what a man is and should be. I can only hope that I will be as good a man."

***

We have seen some wonderful dads—and some dads who confuse, disappoint, or hurt their children. I wanted to leave Rachael's essay for last because it shows the enormous love she has for her dad. Rachael's dad understood what he didn't have when he grew up and was determined to make sure that his children didn't experience similar deprivation. Rachael also cites him as being different from other fathers, a prevalent theme noted quite often in the laudatory essays I have read. In my opinion, her understanding of her father's influence on how she views men is exceptional in a sea of exceptional student essays.

▶ Rachael

"As babies, humans of all cultures are thrown into a melting pot of advice, traditions, and gender-typing. These social constructions help provide a 'normal' map for individuals to follow throughout their lives. One of the strongest images instilled in children is what it means to be a woman and a man. In this culture, we come to learn early on that a man enjoys competition, is aggressive, and is not emotional. But what happens when a child's primary male role-model doesn't fit into the societal mold for men?

My father is not what one imagines when they talk of a 'masculine man.' He's talkative, altruistic, and emotionally expressive. For some, these qualities resonate with a feminine persona rather than a masculine one, but for me my dad is a man. It's when the puzzle piece doesn't fit into the puzzle that you have to alter your approach. For me, having a father who varied from the typical macho image of manliness has redefined what a man is to me.

The beauty of being a child is that social influences are far less apparent than when you get older. It is when you are a teenager and adult that societal norms seem to become an unconscious checklist that is being checked obsessively. When I was a kid, I never gave much thought to my dad being 'different' from other fathers, but as I got older and learned from my friends, I saw that my dad was more of a motherly figure by societal terms than a father. He was actively involved in my education and at home, we often played together and went on errands together; all of the things that my friends' *moms* were doing with them, I was doing with my dad. It wasn't until fourth grade that my personal and societal world collided, forever changing 'man' as I knew it.

It's hard to distinguish societal constructions and personal constructions unless you are actively told. I never thought much of what it meant to be a man when I was younger and still don't; my experiences have shaped my view unconsciously. Although the reality is that society tells you what a man should be and personal experience displays the truth of what men are.

When I was in fourth grade, my dad was the manliest man I knew. I didn't have much to compare him to: I didn't watch much television, and

I lived in a small town. It was only during a class discussion that I began to think of my dad differently. It was a conversation about reading, and while I don't remember the details, I remember telling the small group that my dad loved to read—it was one of his favorite things to do. My peers came crashing down with comments like "Only girls like to read" and "Your dad is a girl." At an age when the concept of intellectuality didn't exist, this was upsetting but not crushing. I didn't realize the magnitude of that comment for many years.

It was living in a small town in New Hampshire that made me realize my dad was different. The fathers of my friends were exactly what society paints men to be. They all held physical jobs like construction and logging, they played on the pick-up sports teams, and they all went to the bar for 'men's night.' My dad worked with stocks, read instead of playing sports, and didn't drink. My dad has always been passive; he's the nice guy. When I got in trouble at school it wasn't my father I was afraid of talking to (like my friends), it was my mother. You could find him chatting to a stranger about the weather or some oddity he just discovered. In the supermarket, instead of walking by the employees he would say hello and ask questions. He got the reputation of being the friendliest stranger you could meet in town.

What seems eye-opening when looking back is that to me my dad was just a dad—he took care of me like other dads, he loved me, and he taught me lessons throughout growing up. Why then is it that my dad seems 'different' from other fathers? Society coats the image of dads as being less-involved parents, as being the supporter of the family not of the individuals in the family. My dad was always there though; his compassion surpassed that of the 'normal' father. He would take time out of his day to take me to get ice cream if I did poorly in school, and come home early from work with a Disney movie I couldn't wait to see. He always seemed to be going out of his way for me. Why is it that a father cannot be actively involved like mothers are? Why are they limited to being distant and in some ways colder to the growing up process? Growing up with a father like mine helped me know that men are not limited to their societal personas; they can be emotional and involved.

It's difficult to say *why* my dad was different. As we learn from our parents, we grow to embody some of their traits and dispel others. I believe that is what happened with my dad. His real father left before he was born, and my grandfather adopted him at birth and raised him with my grandmother. My grandfather was a typical New York City businessman, living on liquid-lunches and constantly busy. He was a good man though; he supported his family with everything they needed and was extremely altruistic in the process. My dad grew up looking up to his father and still does to this day. Behind the scenes, though, my grandfather was a bit different: He often 'forgot' to pick up my dad when he was drinking, and he was too exhausted at the end of the day to play any games with a child. This never altered the love of my dad for his father. But my dad was changed by this in ways he wouldn't notice.

My dad is different from the societal constructions of what a man is. In comparison to cultural views of a man, my dad may be too 'sissy' or 'weak,' but he exerts strength that many men envy. He is strong in knowing he can do anything he cares to. He can read when everyone is playing sports, he can talk to both his daughters and sons about how they are feeling, and he can be as emotional as he wants and know his family is not judging him. Throughout my youth I have learned from my dad that people are different, what may be enjoyable for some isn't for others."

Conclusion

This book is not intended as a condemnation of some fathers nor as a way to put other fathers on pedestals; instead, it simply is my impassioned attempt to convey to readers how much fathers *do* matter and how much words from fathers matter too. My students have taught me that young people are amazingly resilient and that they are capable of taking in the strengths and shortcomings of their fathers (and mothers), and they are remarkably capable of sorting things out and moving on.

In addition, if this book has challenged you in any way to rethink your own behaviors or attitudes about what fatherhood and a "real" man is, or if it has reinforced that you are indeed a good man or father, then the book has met and surpassed my hopes and expectations. Moreover, I would consider it a "real" success.

—"Dr. Dave"

How My Father Influenced My View of a Man

I have decided to include a few pages here to encourage readers to answer some of the questions raised in this book for themselves. These short pages only begin the conversation: true communication breakthroughs come when and if you choose to share what you feel and write with your loved ones—fathers, sons, and daughters.

Questions for sons and daughters

List five things that your father did or said that has influenced your view of a man:

1.

2.

3.

4.

5.

Now prioritize this list. Which of the five things noted has affected you the most? Place an asterisk next to this one. Has the effect been a positive or a negative one? Put a (+) or a (-) to the left of each of the numbers 1–5 as you reflect back on how you have been affected.

Questions for fathers

1. Have you ever asked your son or daughter if he or she is happy with the relationship between the two of you? If you have, what was his or her response? How did you respond? Use the space below to write about how you have or will meet this relationship and communication challenge.

2. Have you ever asked the question "Was I a good father?" If you have asked, to whom? What was their answer, and what answer did you give yourself? Was there a difference? What did you *do* about that answer? Write down below what happened.

3. Are you a "macho" dad? Are you the one who has to be in charge because you know best? Are you the dad who sets the standard for how all men are supposed to act, feel, and behave? Were there times when you wished that your own father were different—not so harsh, uncaring, demanding? On the other hand, did you just accept him? Did you later *become* like him? List below some of the messages you received as a child and then list similar things you have said or done to your children.

4. When was the last time you cried, and was it over something other than a death? Have you ever told your son not to cry? Why? Do you let those who love you see your emotions – including sadness and tears? Are you afraid to show tears? How much energy do you have to expend to keep your emotions in check? Do you make comments when you see men crying in public?

5. If you are a father who is absent from your son or daughter's life, what are you willing to do to change that? What are some of the decisions you have made about how you spend your time that might have affected your children (working late, working too much, missing birthdays, anniversaries, athletic competitions, concerts, recitals, seemingly putting work before your family)? How have you explained your absence to your kids? What can you do today to begin the process of healing? List some of your ideas here.

6. If you are a father and you drink to the point that your drinking interferes with your relationships, work, or physical health, what steps have you taken to deal with this misuse, abuse, or addiction? Are you aware that this behavior destroys relationships and the self-worth of your children? There are many programs and resources available today to help support you in changing this behavior; please list what steps you would be willing to take to deal with the alcohol issues in your life.

7. If you have a son or a daughter who is gay, lesbian, bisexual, or transgendered, have you created a safe home environment where your LGBT child can find the support and love that they will need to survive this all-too-often homophobic society? Have you ever wondered about your own rhetoric on LGBT issues or the rhetoric of your parents or friends? Think of things that are said in your home that are supportive or hurtful of LGBT issues and list them below. (Note: Most communities today have a branch of PFLAG [Parents & Family of Lesbian and Gay kids]—a wonderful resource for families.)

8. Are you one of the "good" dads? What are your good qualities and what do you do that would help make you one of the "good" dads? Although we all have shortcomings and areas that need improvement, in one sense or another, I suggest that we are ALL good dads and want-to-be-better dads.

9. Finally, it might be interesting for you to think about how your son or daughter would answer my challenging question of *How My Father Influenced My View of What a Man Is* when they are talking about *you*. Do you suspect that you would you be saddened, delighted, surprised, or appalled by your son's or daughter's response?

What's Wrong with Me?

Questions for everyone

1. As I have pointed out throughout the book, too many times we have "learned," directly or indirectly, that there is something wrong with us. Perhaps we think we are not good enough, attractive enough, strong enough, a good enough athlete, a good enough student, etc. List some of the "not good enough" messages you still carry; don't worry, you *are* good enough. It is important to understand where some of our earliest messages and false assumptions come from so that we can discard them.

2. List some of your family secrets below. We all have them. Secrets lose their power once you give them voice and write them down. Family secrets are usually not that secret. I have shared some of mine in this book—what are yours?

3. Is your family one that doesn't tell each other "I love you?" Do you assume "we all know that" so you don't need to give voice to this very basic need (to be loved and to know it)? What might the consequences be if you and your family don't express your love? In what ways might you be willing to change this?

References/Reading Suggestions

Black, C. (2001). It will never happen to me: Growing up with addiction as youngsters, adolescents, adults. Bainbridge Island, WA: MAC Publishing

Garcia, G. (2008). The decline of men: How the american male is getting axed, giving up, and flipping off his future. New York, NY: Harper Perennial.

Gurian, M. (1999). The good son: Shaping the moral development of our boys and young men. New York, NY: Tarcher/Putnam.

Gurian, M. (1996). The wonder of boys: what parents, mentors and educators can do to shape boys into exceptional men. New York, NY: Tarcher/Putnam.

Katz. J. (2006). The macho paradox: Why some men hurt women and how all men can help. Naperville, IL: Sourcebooks, Inc.

Kimmel, M. (2008). Guyland. New York, NY: Harper Collins.

Pollack, W. (1998). Real Boys : Rescuing our sons from the myths of boyhood. New York, NY: Henry Holt.

Pope, Jr., H. G., Phillips, K. A., & Olivardia, R. (2000). *The adonis complex: how to identify, treat, and prevent body obsession in men and boys.* New York, New York: Simon & Schuster.

Real, T. (1997). I don't want to talk about it. New York, NY: Simon & Schuster.

Tessier, B. (2010). The Intentional father: adventures in adoptive single parenting. Boston, MA: Xlibris Corp.